# Fashion Speak

## DAVID MEAGHER

RANDOM HOUSE AUSTRALIA

Random House Australia Pty Ltd
Level 3, 100 Pacific Highway, North Sydney, NSW 2060
www.randomhouse.com.au

Sydney   New York   Toronto
London   Auckland   Johannesburg

First published by Random House Australia 2008

National Library of Australia
Cataloguing-in-Publication Entry

Meagher, David, 1966–.
Fashion speak: interviews with the world's leading fashion designers.
ISBN 978 1 74166 499 7

Fashion designers.
Fashion designers – Interviews.
Fashion designers – Biography.
Fashion design.
Fashion shows.
Fashion merchandising.

746.920922

Cover illustration and design by Natalie Winter
Internal design by Natalie Winter
Typeset in Centaur MT 13/18
Author photograph by Kane Skennar
Manufactured/printed in Singapore by Imago

10 9 8 7 6 5 4 3 2 1

David Meagher is the editor of *Wish* magazine in *The Australian* newspaper. He has written extensively on fashion and design and was previously a staff writer and fashion editor on *The Australian Financial Review Magazine* for seven years. His first book, *It's Not Etiquette: A Guide to Modern Manners*, was published by Random House in 2005. He lives in Sydney.

# CONTENTS

# INTRODUCTION

I have had always had an interest in fashion. In fact my earliest memories are associated, in my mind, with what I was wearing when the event took place.

I remember vividly going shopping with my mother at the Sydney department store David Jones when I must have been just five years old. We had been to see the ophthalmologist, something we did regularly in those days because I had a lazy eye problem. As was usual on these trips, it was just me and my mother. My brothers were either at home with my grandmother or at school. My mother had a firm belief in those days that when you went into 'the city' – meaning the Sydney CBD – you wore your best clothes. It was an occasion, even if it was just for a medical appointment, and deserved my best shoes, my older brother's itchy navy wool shorts and matching jacket. The message was clear: the clothes I had in my wardrobe were not suitable for an outing of such magnitude.

Despite looking pretty sharp in my brother's clothes I was far from comfortable, and it wasn't just the itchy fabric. Nothing fit right. The jacket and the pants were too big. Not so big they were falling off me, but big enough for me to be self-conscious about what I was wearing. I felt as though everyone we passed in the street was saying to themselves: 'What a stylish-looking woman and a handsome young boy, but, oh dear, what a shame those clothes don't fit him.'

So I fidgeted and squirmed all morning on the bus and while sitting in the waiting room at the ophthalmologist, much to my mother's annoyance. She must have caught sight of the two of us in a shop window at one point and thought to herself what everyone else was thinking about my attire, because after the doctor's appointment she took me to the boys department to buy me some new clothes. Intent on resting her feet by this stage, she told me that I could pick out one good outfit. This was about 1970, so I chose an olive green pair of corduroy pants and a purple cable knit jumper and, yes, I wore them together and would have been happy wearing them everywhere. I knew I looked good and was very happy with my decisions. When my mother paid for them she asked me not to mention the purchase to my father and not to parade around in my new clothes when I got home.

I think it was at that point that I first saw buying clothes as an act that should be private and hidden and associated it with a feeling of joy that was hard to describe. I was the middle child of five boys and I loathed having to wear my brothers' clothes, but in a big family hand-me-downs were a fact of life. At the age of just five I had become one of the fashion industry's most sought-after consumers: one who takes pleasure in buying something new when they don't really need it and who appreciates the intangible value beautiful clothes have. Not to mention one who couldn't afford what they really wanted, strictly speaking, but purchased it anyway.

When I first left school I planned to be an architect, but when that didn't quite work out I fell into a field in which I felt I had some expertise: I became a shop assistant for the Australian clothing brand Country Road, a position I held for almost six years. This was the mid 1980s and the Country Road brand was in its heyday. It was a fun place to work and I still have friends who I met working there. Perhaps the most appealing aspect of the job, however, was the staff discount. We had to wear the brand during work hours, of course, but I had no problem wearing Country Road outside of work too. I was a true believer. I loved it when the new season stock would arrive and we'd unpack it — and suddenly I'd have no interest in selling last season's clothes. The training we received at Country Road was first-rate and involved not just customer service, but an education about how clothes are made and how they should fit.

Though it took several years, the gloss eventually wore off the job — standing on your feet all day and getting a customer's suit to fit properly is not all that intellectually stimulating, after all. After years of working with the one brand, of talking about clothes all day long, of folding endless jumpers, and pinning what seemed like a million hems, I decided I wanted to work as far away from fashion as possible. Eating, sleeping and breathing fashion had taken all the fun out of it.

So I went back to university and started studying to become a journalist, which had originally been my second choice when I finished high school. After graduating I became a freelance writer, figuring it would be the best way to get some experience under my belt and would eventually lead to a full-time position. A journalist friend of mine told me that I needed to have a speciality and not just write about anything and everything, so I decided to write about subjects I felt I knew a bit about: architecture and fashion. A couple of years later I was offered a position as a staff writer on *The Australian Financial Review Magazine*, and when the opportunity arose in 2000 to become the magazine's fashion editor I jumped at it.

I was working in a field that I love – journalism – and writing about an area in which I had some expertise. Working for a paper such as *The Australian Financial Review* meant that I was required to go a little deeper into the fashion industry, not just focusing on hemlines and fabric colours. In fact I did very little of that sort of writing and was often at a loss when I was asked to give my opinion on a collection. Instead I approached the fashion industry as a serious business and looked at corporate trends rather than aesthetic ones. My tenure at the *AFR* coincided with a period of globalisation in the fashion industry that saw old, often family-owned businesses gobbled up by major conglomerates. While some people might have decried the developments in the industry, there's no doubt that it made writing about it that much more interesting.

A colleague once told me that fashion journalism was an oxymoron. It probably comes as no surprise to a punter to learn that fashion journalists have an image problem within their own professional ranks. Many people seem to imagine that they spend their time going to function after function, sipping champagne all day, and then type out a few nice words. Fashion journalists are thought of as uncritical of the businesses they report on and it's assumed that their allegiance can be bought with free handbags and business class airfares (and to be fair, some of them can be, and are). In a newsroom a fashion reporter is commonly viewed as a convenient tool used to cosy up to big-spending fashion advertisers.

And therein lies a great irony: despite the veneer of frivolity, fashion advertisers have enormous marketing budgets, because they are players in a major global industry. Take the world's largest luxury fashion company as an example: the Paris-based Moët Hennessy–Louis Vuitton (LVMH). LVMH owns a portfolio of high-fashion brands, including Louis Vuitton, Christian Dior, Kenzo, Givenchy, Marc Jacobs, Donna Karan and Fendi, and has interests in several wine and spirit brands, cosmetics, watches and jewellery.

Compare LVMH – for all intents and purposes a fashion company – to Australia's biggest company, BHP Billiton, or the 'Big Australian' as it is colloquially known. For the twelve months to 30 June 2007, BHP Billiton reported revenue of US$23.06 billion. Over roughly the same period, LVMH reported revenue of €15.3 billion, or US$20.4 billion at exchange rates current at the time of publication.

Just as BHP Billiton needs to plan for growth and have strategies in place to ensure the longevity of the business and a return for its shareholders, so too must a company like LVMH. And LVMH is not an isolated case. PPR (or Pinault-Printemps-Redoute, as it was formerly known) is a French company listed on Euronext Paris. Among other interests, it owns the Gucci Group – the umbrella company for fashion brands such as Yves Saint Laurent, Stella McCartney, Balenciaga, Bottega Veneta and Alexander McQueen. Then there's Hermès, which owns Jean Paul Gaultier and the shoe brand John Lobb. Hermès is relative minnow in comparison to LVMH but still managed to generate €1.5 billion in revenue in 2006. For the six months to 30 June 2007 revenue was up by 3 per cent to €721 million. England's Burberry is now listed on the London Stock Exchange and for the twelve months to 31 March 2007 had revenue of £850.3 million. With numbers like that there's a lot more at stake in the fashion business today than skirt lengths and finding new names for age-old colours.

Like BHP Billiton, companies such as LVMH need to increase their market and sell more goods as well as finding cheaper ways to produce those goods without compromising quality. But unlike the resources giant, fashion brands also need to maintain their 'it' factor if they are to grow. Their stock in trade is intellectual property and the creative ability of their designers to meet consumer demand, season after season, for original clothes and beautiful shoes and must-have handbags and so on. These shoes, clothes and handbags must be unlike the ones the competition is producing, must be luxurious, and must have the magic ability to make someone feel happy and good about themselves. Can coal do that?

Purely as a big business the fashion industry is worthy of study. As a big business that produces goods which have both a monetary value and an intangible one, it's all the more interesting. In the profiles in this book I explore the tension that exists between a designer's creativity and the need to make a profit; between the production of art and the need for growth. I spoke to designers such as Marc Jacobs, Christopher Bailey and Nicole and Michael Colovos who work for large multinational corporations, but this book also includes interviews with designers working outside the luxury goods system, including Akira Isogawa, Josh Goot, Martin Grant and Karen Walker. While they are not part of the big-brand system, these individuals still have to balance creativity and commercial pressures in order to run viable businesses and make a living. Many have silent financial partners — and partners who invest money in a business, no matter how 'silent' they are, or how critically acclaimed the designer is, will at some stage want to see a return on their investment.

Fashion is about change. What's in one season can be out the next, or it can be part of an evolving story. On the catwalk, it's about newness, a revolution each season. And in a business sense the industry is no less fickle. In the course of writing this book one of the designers I'd interviewed, Hedi Slimane, left his job at Dior, citing irreconcilable differences with his employer, the luxury conglomerate LVMH. Another design partnership I was planning to write about, Trovata, broke up.

In 2000, Slimane created Dior Homme — the menswear offshoot of Christian Dior — from scratch, and turned it into the biggest force in men's fashion in decades. He was arguably the hottest designer on the planet and I spent a great deal of energy hunting him down and securing an interview with him. Then in March 2007, with no other job to go to, Slimane decided to leave Dior Homme at its peak.

Like Slimane, the American design collective Trovata caused a huge fuss when they first arrived on the scene. Four surfer dudes,

John Whitledge, Sam Shipley, Jeff Halmos and Josia Lamberto-Egan, formed the label while still in college, with no fashion experience. They became that elusive thing the fashion business prizes: an overnight sensation. Everything looked on the up for the four, especially after they won the prestigious Council of Fashion Designers of America/ *Vogue* Fashion Fund award of US$200,000 in 2005. On a visit to Australia that year the four boys agreed to an interview: they painted a rosy picture of how they all worked together, explaining that they'd located their office near the beach so they could surf if the mood took them and describing their plans for world domination. Less than a year later three of the four had left the business and John Whitledge had become a solo act. Jeff Halmos and Sam Shipley have now gone out on their own and started a new fashion company, Shipley & Halmos.

I made the decision to include Hedi Slimane's profile in this book and to cut the interview I did with the four Trovata boys, for the simple reason that I have no doubt Slimane will surface again in a major way. At Dior Slimane proved he was bigger than the hype. He has the most singular approach to fashion of any designer working today, and the most identifiable handwriting. Trovata, on the other hand, made its name with a laid-back preppy style that had many competitors and rival brands. There's no doubt that the Trovata boys are talented designers and businessmen, but my conviction that Slimane will go on to greater things is far stronger. He sees fashion as a total lifestyle, one that encompasses not only clothing but also architecture, photography and music — all disciplines he has experimented with. He has been known to seek inspiration from the rock music scene and told me when we spoke: 'Music is all there is. I just would not do anything without it.'

Slimane knows that fashion is not so much about who you are as who you want to be. And if that point needed underlining, the Boston-based rock band Keys to the Streets of Fear did it when they recorded the song 'Hedi Slimane' in 2005. The song features lyrics such as 'I want pants like Hedi Slimane' and 'I want jeans like Hedi Slimane', followed by the chorus 'I want to fuck like Hedi Slimane.'

I don't necessarily want to do what the Keys to the Streets of Fear want to do, but I think they have a point: how we dress defines who we are. You don't really need to be part of the indie rock scene to look like you belong in it. Buy the clothes and carry the look off and that's all that matters. Fashion has the power to transform us, as the popularity of reality TV makeover shows attests. Clothes give us our character and say something about who we are, who we think we are, and who we would like to be. Like it or not, even the most diehard opponents of fashion make decisions each day about what they are going to wear — if only to show the world that they don't care.

I should confess that my interest in fashion is not purely journalistic. I spend way too much money on clothes and I do this even though I've watched the industry closely over the years and have seen the enormous margins fashion brands make. What motivated me to write this book was a desire to discover how fashion designers put together their collections each season and what inspires them. After all, they're the people who give us the palette we choose from when getting dressed in the morning.

MARC JACOBS

If there is one fashion designer who personifies the friction between art and commerce – and does it successfully – it's Marc Jacobs.

Jacobs has his own eponymous label, but he is also the designer of the Louis Vuitton brand, the cash cow of the French luxury goods juggernaut Moët Hennessy–Louis Vuitton (LVMH). He is responsible for the look and feel of almost all the products that bear the Louis Vuitton marque.

In addition to Louis Vuitton, LVMH owns prestige fashion brands such as Fendi, Givenchy, Kenzo and Donna Karan; liquor brands such as Moët & Chandon, Veuve Clicquot, Krug, Cape Mentelle and Cloudy Bay; watch brands such as Tag Heuer and Zenith; and retailers such as DFS and Le Bon Marché, making it not just the largest luxury conglomerate in the world, but one of France's biggest companies – bigger than Renault and Peugeot, and almost as big as France Telecom. While Jacobs is the designer of just one of its brands, it's one hell of a brand. LVMH does not break down results for its individual brands, but luxury goods analysts estimate that Louis Vuitton is responsible for 60 per cent of LVMH's profits. In 2006, for example, the group recorded operating profits of €3.1 billion based on revenue of €15.3 billion. This indicates that Louis Vuitton's revenue is almost twice that of rival brands such as Gucci and Prada.

With the success of the conglomerate relying so heavily on the continued growth of one brand, you'd think the LVMH management would choose a 'safe' designer to steer the label, right? Think again. Safe is not an adjective that people typically use to describe Marc Jacobs. The word they use is, more often than not, 'cool'.

In fact, it seems to be the only word people use when they have to pick one that best sums him up. Consider the title of every major recent magazine profile of him. UK *Vogue* dubbed him 'Cool Hand Marc'. *Time* referred to Jacobs's 'School of Cool', *New York* magazine crowned him 'fashion's coolest, most influential designer', and *The Wall Street Journal* described him as 'the epitome of laid-back cool', leaving *Vanity Fair* with nowhere to go. 'He's not just cool, he's so fucking cool,' the magazine opined.

But 'cool' is in fact only an approximation of the quality that sets Jacobs apart. He may be the creative brain of a major luxury goods house, but Jacobs retains something of the wild from which he came. His edge is his edginess. He was certainly a risky hire back in 1997 when the chairman of LVMH, Bernard Arnault, hand-picked him to launch a ready-to-wear line for the venerable house of Louis Vuitton. At the time, Jacobs was considered a critical success but a commercial disaster, as famous for his partying as his clothes. The latter had made him notorious, not least the grunge collection that had seen him sacked from the American label Perry Ellis a few years earlier. Jacobs was also as New York as the Empire State Building, and Louis Vuitton as French as the Eiffel Tower.

But it worked. In hiring Jacobs, Louis Vuitton was buying some of his cred and giving the once-staid brand much-needed cool — which has since translated into serious heat at the cash register. Since his arrival, Louis Vuitton's overall sales have grown from US$1.2 billion in 1997 to US$2.4 billion in 2001 and on to US$3.8 billion in 2006, according to analysts' reports.

Jacobs's *annus mirabilis* was 2001, the year in which he collaborated with the New York artist Stephen Sprouse to radically update the Louis Vuitton monogram print. The result, the graffiti bag, proved an instant bestseller and was followed in 2003 by Jacobs's collaboration with the Japanese artist Takashi Murakami. The Murakami bag, too, was a hit, accounting for US$345 million in sales, or roughly 10 per cent of the total Louis Vuitton revenue for that year. Jacobs is now acknowledged as the master of the 'it' handbag – the profit engine of today's luxury goods business. For autumn/winter 2007, Jacobs, in his tenth year at Louis Vuitton, designed a Dutch Masters–inspired collection, cleverly titled 'Girl with a Monogram Handbag'.

And alongside the must-have handbags, Jacobs has continued to produce consistently elegant, commercially successful ready-to-wear collections.

With the kind of money at stake that companies such as Louis Vuitton generate, it's little wonder that today's fashion designers tend to sound more like suits than artists. They've been management schooled and media trained until they only open their mouths to 'reinforce brand values', particularly when speaking to journalists.

But Jacobs's title – artistic director, rather than the more business-like 'head designer' – is no accident. And he's refreshingly frank about his lack of interest in the business of his art:

I'm pretty shielded from that. I'm not a business person so I don't really like getting involved in conversations about business and numbers. Thankfully I'm not really asked to participate in those conversations all that much. The fact that it's a real business is a bit of a con sometimes, I guess. Things have to be done somewhat on schedule which is always a difficult thing for creative people. It's not like you can make the decision to wake up tomorrow and be creative.

There's always a show [to prepare for] and there's always another show coming and you have to be there and show up.

It's an interesting balancing act: a listed company, a huge international business based on the riskiest, least predictable commodity — cutting-edge creativity. Asked about those big-selling bag collaborations, Jacobs says: 'My choice in collaborating with different people just comes from my heart. It's not like I can make the Murakami moment happen again.'

While that might be enough to send a bean counter into a panic, Jacobs's nonchalance is, of course, another of the secrets of his success. His friend Sofia Coppola, daughter of Francis Ford Coppola and director of *Lost in Translation*, described the appeal of his clothes to *The Wall Street Journal* in 2004. 'He doesn't take things too seriously. It's chic but not too done. You look together and not uncomfortable,' she said. In other words, Jacobs makes his customers look like they, too, aren't trying too hard. He also has an uncanny knack of sensing today what people will want to wear tomorrow. 'Great designers . . . intuit the next mood; they identify a culture's swirling undercurrents. Jacobs has always known where the wind is blowing next,' US *Vogue* said of the designer in September 2005.

Jacobs is a designer who can shift direction radically from season to season — throwing out all he believes one moment for something entirely different the next. His winter 2005 Louis Vuitton collection, for example, was moody, full of dark colours and lush romanticism. It was almost an extension of the grunge revival he had shown for his own collection a few weeks earlier. At the following round of collection shows, for spring/summer 2006, Jacobs appeared to be going back to the 1980s. The Louis Vuitton collection was all fluoro colours, short skirts, gold chains and razzle dazzle. There were wild prints and graphic patterns. After the show Jacobs said, 'Happy, happy fashion – there is not much more to it than that.' By autumn/winter 2007, he was back to beautiful tailoring and luxurious, wearable clothes.

Jacobs makes no secret of the fact that his relationship with his friends influences the design of his clothes, and this makes him stand out from the pack. It seems that every fashion season, designers offer up this person or that person as the inspiration for their collection, without having any real connection with the individual in question, but Jacobs's approach is to design for the people he spends his time with. He stops short, however, of singling out one of these friends as a sort of muse.

I don't really sit down at the beginning of each season and try and figure out who this elusive muse is. But at some point in the creative process I go through a series of questions in my head. Is this for someone who exists today? Is there someone I can think of who would wear something like this? I think that process makes me believe that something is credible or has a reason to be. I like to know that there is someone I can think of who would like to wear whatever it is I am designing.

Of course, all that legendary nonchalance is high maintenance. I interviewed Jacobs at Hong Kong's Four Seasons Hotel; when he arrived for the press conference, he was flanked by half a dozen of his own people, including his impossibly chic right-hand woman, Camille Miceli. Miceli, who formerly worked in the public relations department at that other bastion of French chic, Chanel, came to Louis Vuitton as a public relations director; today she designs the house's jewellery line and, as one insider puts it, 'manages' Jacobs's personal image. She's a sort of type-A alter ego to all that cool.

It's barely breakfast time and Miceli is runway ready in a red Louis Vuitton jersey dress from the previous season's collection and fantastically high purple suede shoes, her dark hair swept into a neat chignon, her face immaculately made up.

Despite the fact that Jacobs designed everything Miceli is wearing, his own equally signature look suggests he's strayed in from some more ordinary galaxy: nondescript black trousers, simple navy sweater, plain white shirt and knocked-about white adidas trainers. His shoulder-length hair is unkempt, as you would expect at this hour of the morning after a party the night before, and his trademark clear plastic spectacles frame tired-looking eyes. 'I wish I could look really smart and chic,' the 44-year-old laments at the start of our interview, after ordering a Diet Coke and firing up the first of many Marlboro Lights.

> There are all these designers like Karl Lagerfeld or John Galliano or Tom Ford, they have such a strong look, and I just can't do that. I can't wake up that early and have hair and make-up and all that. I just want to put on the same shoes and not think or worry about it, and cheap socks and clean underwear. I just want to be comfortable and able to do things and I don't really care too much about how I look. I wish I cared more, but I just don't.

His approach has changed somewhat since then: in 2007 Jacobs discovered the gym and started dressing to show off his new physique. Despite this, he still has 'a funny relationship with men's fashion'.

> Menswear is a weird thing for me to talk about because I don't really like it. I understand that men, like women, do love fashion. Guys want new shoes and bags and belts and whatever else. It's as important to many men as it is to many women. I keep meeting different guys and I'm so amazed at how obsessed with things in fashion they are, like sunglasses and jewellery and watches, and I just think 'Wow, that's so weird' . . . I mean, you're talking to someone who wears the same sneakers and same sweater every day. I just don't get it, but thank God they do.

Little wonder his minders seem to hold their collective breath as Jacobs answers questions. His frankness is disarming, not least on the fraught issue of counterfeiting. So how does he feel about all those knock-off Louis Vuitton bags out there?

> I know Louis Vuitton as a company doesn't feel very good about that. In fact, they have tons of people to find counterfeiters and harass them and all that. But I find as a designer . . . when we've done things like our collaboration with Takashi Murakami, which has launched a lot of wannabes and copies, my team and I were very proud that something we did had such an impact . . . when you do something that people want and covet . . . as a creative person, I see that as a form of flattery.

Little in Jacob's early career suggested a billion-dollar designer in the making — save a talent that was, from the start, as precocious as it was prodigious. Born in 1964 into a middle-class family on New York's Upper West Side, he was the child of parents who both worked for William Morris, the talent and literary agency. He has rarely gone on the record about his upbringing, except to say that he left home at an early age, has little contact with his siblings and was raised by his grandmother, who was something of an Auntie Mame figure in his life. In early interviews Jacobs talked about how she took him shopping at New York's up-market department stores and encouraged him in his career.

By the time he'd graduated from the Parsons School of Design in New York City in 1984, Jacobs had already sold his first collection – hand-knitted sweaters with smiley faces on them – to the hip Upper West Side boutique Charivari. His graduation show caught the eye of Robert Duffy, sales manager at the clothing manufacturer Reuben Thomas, who immediately offered Jacobs a job designing the Sketchbook label.

Today, Duffy remains Jacobs's business partner: a dynamic reminiscent of other legendary fashion double acts from Yves Saint Laurent and Pierre Bergé to Tom Ford and Domenico De Sole at Gucci.

By 1988, Jacobs, still just twenty-five, had been named womenswear designer for Perry Ellis; Duffy became the company's president. Perry Ellis was a US$700-million-a-year business at the time. Ellis, who had died two years earlier, had been famous for the playfulness and whimsy of his American sportswear collections – 'easy-dressing' as it was known. Models often skipped down the Perry Ellis runway. Jacobs set about injecting energy and excitement back into the brand.

And it worked, initially at least. Jacobs's first collections were well received – until that infamous autumn/winter 1992 collection, inspired by the grunge music scene generally and rock'n'roll friends such as Kim Gordon of Sonic Youth in particular. What Jacobs

invented was grunge luxe: lots of cashmere, silk dresses teamed with thermals and accessorised with work boots and knitted skullcaps. The press was outraged that Jacobs had reeled in a look from the fringes of fashion and sent it down the runway, with *The New York Times* dubbing it 'a mess'. At Perry Ellis, executives stopped production and summarily sacked Jacobs. Today, with the benefit of hindsight, the same publications praise the collection as visionary. Jacobs has certainly had the last laugh. During his tenure at Perry Ellis, he hired the then-unknown Tom Ford as the creative force behind the Perry Ellis jeans line – who went on not only to reinvent Gucci but also to personify the era of the star designer.

The upshot was that Jacobs and Duffy decided to go it alone, setting up Marc Jacobs International (MJI) in 1993. The fashion press loved the label and supermodels Kate Moss, Christy Turlington and Naomi Campbell routinely did Jacobs shows for free. But despite the critical success, Jacobs remained a fringe figure in fashion, and the retail space the pair rented on Mercer Street in New York's SoHo would remain empty for about four years. There was no money to fit it out. Distribution was limited and sales amounted to only US$2.6 million by 1996. To stave off bankruptcy, Duffy mortgaged his house. The business would continue to be a seat-of-the-pants operation until a knight in shining armour, Bernard Arnault of LVMH, rode into New York in 1997.

Arnault, who had owned Louis Vuitton since 1989, was on a shopping spree, gobbling up an array of French luxury brands including Christian Dior, Givenchy, Kenzo and Christian Lacroix. Now he was looking for a designer to expand Louis Vuitton's luggage and accessories business into ready-to-wear clothing. Somewhat amazingly, Jacobs had come onto Arnault's radar and, following a drawn-out courtship, he offered Jacobs the job.

It was Duffy who convinced Arnault to back MJI as part of the deal. LVMH agreed to underwrite the business so that it could produce two fashion shows a year, and immediately stumped up US$140,000 for renovations to the SoHo store. By 2004, LVMH had invested more than US$50 million in the Marc Jacobs business, and today the company owns 96 per cent of MJI. Along the way, Jacobs moved to Paris, where designing Louis Vuitton would become his first priority, while Duffy remained in New York to run the Marc Jacobs brand.

But even with a dream job in a dream city and the backing of a huge French conglomerate, the road ahead proved anything but smooth. At around the time he started at Louis Vuitton, Jacobs developed a major drug habit. He would skip work for weeks at a time, miss important meetings and get thrown off aeroplanes.

Jacobs explains:

I would come into work and fall straight asleep. Then I would tell everyone to come in on Saturday because we were behind, and then I wouldn't show up.

Duffy attempted to cover for him, but things were uneasy.

The Louis Vuitton style was also very different from Jacobs's own, and he struggled with it in the early days. Mounting tensions with Louis Vuitton executives came to a head over a humble scarf. Jacobs wanted to include a group of scarves in boiled cashmere – which would look more like Shetland wool and was designed to pill with age – in his first collection. It was a characteristically devil-may-care gesture. 'Ideally, it would look a little bit fucked-up – beautiful, but fucked-up,' he told *The New Yorker*. Problem was, Arnault and others knew that the women who shopped at Louis Vuitton didn't necessarily want to look fucked-up.

In September 1997, Jacobs and Duffy vented their frustrations with the firm in a *New Yorker* magazine profile. Not only did they dump on the French way of doing business, they also discussed internal tensions around the creation of Jacobs's Louis Vuitton ready-to-wear line. In the article Jacobs and Duffy described – in detail – meetings they had had with Bernard Arnault and Louis Vuitton boss Yves Carcelle. In one particular meeting, Carcelle gave them the bad news that the renovations to several Louis Vuitton stores to accommodate the new ready-to-wear line might not be ready in time and suggested that some sweaters that Jacobs had designed could just be used the following season. Jacobs responded, 'It won't be the right thing. These sweaters are timely. They're right for this fall. It's fashion.'

The designer could barely conceal his frustration, according to the author of the *New Yorker* piece, and Carcelle is portrayed as being, horror of horrors for a Frenchman, ignorant of fashion.

Arnault and other senior management at LVMH were infuriated. Today, an older and wiser Jacobs regrets the dummy spit. 'People were mad,' he says. 'That article gave us a scarlet letter.'

The *New Yorker* article also reinforced the widespread impression that Jacobs was a risky choice to steer the nearly 150-year-old luggage-maker into the future. Eventually, though, Jacobs would come to accept the principle of different strokes for different folks.

When I first started working here I thought, 'Why would people want Louis Vuitton luggage?' and I thought about it for a very long time. It's not the most practical luggage in the world, or the lightest weight, but it is the most identifiable. When a Louis Vuitton bag comes off the luggage carousel at the airport, everyone knows that it's Louis Vuitton and anybody who has been into the shop knows that it costs a certain price and that it has a certain cachet. So we kind of keep that in mind with the clothes. We think, right, well, if a woman is wearing something from Louis Vuitton, then she kind of wants the world to maybe not [necessarily] know that it's from Louis Vuitton, but [to know] that it's something from *somewhere* and that it has a sort of a gloss . . . that it says *this is something*. And that really is the reverse of what I do with my own collection.

What I do for my own collection is very personal and the choices I make are very personal. I don't really detach myself from them. They are an extension of me and my life and my friends . . . clothes that have a casual attitude about them in some way. But at Louis Vuitton I'm an employee and it's not my name on the door. I'm just a contributor, so I kind of get to role-play with a fantasy. At Louis Vuitton, for example, I think the clothes are much more showy and slightly extroverted – they are for someone who wants to be noticed.

Despite his problems – both personal and professional – Jacobs's collections for Louis Vuitton have been an unqualified commercial success. They have transformed Louis Vuitton from a luggage-maker to one of the most fashionable labels around. Who cared if Jacobs had a drug habit if the tills were ringing? Thankfully Duffy did and persuaded him that his lifestyle might not be so great for him in the long term. Since he famously kicked his habit, his collections have gone from strength to strength. Sobriety has not dulled Jacobs creatively.

Business-wise, however, it hasn't been entirely smooth sailing. Despite the overall success of the partnership, tensions between Louis Vuitton and its artistic director surfaced again in 2004. The principal grievance was that LVMH was neglecting the Marc Jacobs brand and not remunerating Jacobs and Duffy adequately. Each was paid less than US$1 million annually. 'I think Gucci treated Tom Ford better than LVMH has treated me,' Jacobs told *The Wall Street Journal* at the time of his contract negotiations, which saw stock options added to his package as part of a ten-year extension of his contract.

That extension means Jacobs is with Louis Vuitton until at least 2014. But even if he weren't, the company insists it would more than survive. The former managing director, Serge Brunschwig (now CEO of the LVMH-owned Celine brand), points out that Louis Vuitton has a range of classic products that continue to sell well despite not being designed by Jacobs. In fact, he says, it's the basic strength of the Louis Vuitton brand that allows Jacobs his creative freedom:

> Marc creates excellent leather goods, excellent shoes, excellent ready-to-wear, linked to fashion, linked to *l'air du temps* – to what he wants to express at a certain moment. Meaning that we can allow Marc to create very freely because the profit and the fate of the company don't rely entirely on this.

Antoine Colonna, a luxury goods analyst with Merrill Lynch in Paris, agrees. 'Look at Gucci: it did not die when Tom Ford departed.'

Either way, Jacobs says he's still enjoying the ride. He says it remains:

> . . . a great privilege to be part of the fashion community and to have the opportunity to express myself and do the things that I love to do.

Jacobs's appreciation of the unbending laws of chic can only have been helped by the fact that he has become the quintessential American in Paris. He now calls the city home and lives in the fashionable seventh arrondissement with his two dogs. He explains:

> I wasn't born in Europe and I'm not French, so I'm like this typical New Yorker in Paris and I see things not entirely through realistic glasses.

In Paris, he experiments with European craftsmanship and tradition for Vuitton, and in New York produces clothes more like a dressmaker. In Paris, he designs for people who want to be noticed for what they are wearing – a Camille Miceli type – and in New York, he designs for people who prize understatement. As Sofia Coppola says, 'I like that when you wear his clothes you can't tell it's Marc Jacobs.'

Today, he has more than twenty-five stores worldwide bearing his name as well as the diffusion line Marc by Marc Jacobs. In Australia, his clothes are sold in selected boutiques and David Jones stores nationally. One analyst estimates that the Marc Jacobs brand today would have an annual turnover of approximately US$100 million.

When I spoke to him in 2005, Jacobs said he enjoyed the creativity and workload his sobriety had made possible, but in 2007, he checked himself back into rehab. Duffy told *Women's Wear Daily*:

> He'd been sober for seven years. When he relapsed, he wanted to deal with it right away. According to the experts, such a relapse isn't uncommon. Thankfully, Marc recognized the problem himself and chose to deal with it. Obviously, our prayers are with him.

The confirmation that Jacobs was at a treatment facility came on the day that he received two nominations from the Council of Fashion Designers of America for its upcoming awards. He was nominated in the womenswear and accessories categories.

Post-rehab, Jacobs looks better and healthier than he ever has. Gone is his signature unkempt hair – he now sports a short cropped style. He's fit and tanned, and at the end of his fashion shows, when he takes his bow, he appears to be happy and enjoying it.

He sees this enjoyment as a precondition of success.

> I allow myself and everyone else around me to have fun and indulge themselves in whatever they find they're good at. It's important not

to take it all too seriously, because when you take it very seriously in terms of creating the individual things they tend to be too precious or dull.

And then a line that could only come from Marc Jacobs: 'We like to have fun with it because, in the end, it's not a cure for cancer – it's just fashion.'

# CHRISTOPHER BAILEY

## BURBERRY

In almost every magazine profile on Christopher Bailey, the creative director of the British label Burberry, the same quote appears. When journalists ask him what he likes and what he dislikes (as they tend to do), Bailey responds by saying that he 'just can't bear it when people are pretending to be something they're not'.

He said it to British *Vogue* in February 2006, when asked to describe his fascination with the model Stella Tennant.

> What I like about Stella is that she is without pretension. I can't bear
> it when people are trying to be something that they're not.

Tennant, Burberry's house model, doesn't really need to pretend, of course: she's the granddaughter of the Duke and Duchess of Devonshire. The duchess was one of the Mitford sisters and a fourth cousin of Diana, Princess of Wales.

Only a few months earlier, in September 2005, Bailey wrote about his love of the artist David Hockney in an article in the UK's *Independent Magazine*: 'You never feel like you have to try and find the meaning of his painting. It's completely unpretentious.'

It's an unusual stance for a fashion designer. Fashion thrives on pretence. It's an industry that sells fantasy and illusion, an industry that has the power to transform people's appearance. On one level fashion is just the rag trade — the design and manufacture of clothing — but it also allows people to pretend that they're something they're not.

No contemporary fashion label illustrates the tension between pretension and utility, between costume and dress, better than Burberry. Consider the brand's heritage: the company was founded by Thomas Burberry in 1856 in Basingstoke, Hampshire, in England, and quickly grew into an emporium specialising in clothing for the outdoors. Burberry, however, was interested in more than just selling clothes; he wanted to improve their functionality as well. In 1880 he developed a breathable, weatherproof and tear-proof fabric which became known as gabardine. In 1895 he designed the Tielocken coat, which was worn by British officers during the Boer War. In 1914 he adapted it for the new combat requirements of World War I and created the trench coat, which is still in production today and is the backbone of the brand's fortunes.

The classic Burberry trench coat quickly made the transition from utility to fashion when it got a starring role on the backs of actors Humphrey Bogart and Ingrid Bergman in the film *Casablanca*. It was subsequently worn by Audrey Hepburn in *Breakfast at Tiffany's* and Peter Sellers in the *Pink Panther* films, proving that the popularity of the trench coat knows no bounds. In real life it has been worn by everyone from Queen Elizabeth II to the 1960s 'it' girl Twiggy; from Sid Vicious, the legendary bass player in the punk band the Sex Pistols, to the model Kate Moss. Throughout its history it has been a status symbol, a badge of rebellion and a disguise – sometimes all at the same time – making it the perfect garment for someone who wants to pretend to be something they're not.

This heritage continues to underpin the brand's remarkable success and informs every collection Yorkshire-born Bailey designs in his role as creative director for Burberry.

> The trench coat is something that I base pretty much every collection on. It can have so many different attitudes and so many different personalities. It can be worn in so many different ways and by so many different types of people. It can be very formal, or very casual, or very fashionable.

Since joining Burberry in 2001, at the age of thirty, Bailey has reinvented the classic Burberry trench coat in myriad ways, from short sexed-up versions to shiny quilted leather styles, from soft silk taffeta to classic men's hound's-tooth. There have been light, white versions as well as heavier renditions, such as the winter 2005 style which fused the trench with a kilt by adding kick pleats for a fuller silhouette. With each new interpretation of the trench coat, Bailey has given it a new life and a new audience.

Bailey says he thinks of the trench coat as a democratic item of clothing, much like a pair of jeans. Its appeal, he says, is not that it is a status symbol or a disguise, but rather that it is a blank canvas and can be worn by people from all walks of life.

> It's literally for everybody. It's the way that you wear it, the attitude that you wear it with. I always liken the trench coat to jeans because like jeans it can be worn by young people, by old people, by very formal or sartorial people and by very casual and relaxed people. It really depends on the person and how they are wearing the trench coat and it almost takes on that life.

The so-called democratic essence of the trench coat has enabled Bailey to play up and down the British class system in designing Burberry's ready-to-wear line, Burberry Prorsum, shown on the catwalks of Milan. (*Prorsum*, which is Latin for 'forwards', was the chosen motto of Thomas Burberry and once appeared on the flag carried by the knight in the company's logo.) In his collections,

Bailey has drawn on a changing cast of upper-crust British personalities from the Duchess of Windsor to David Hockney, and fused their personal style with his modern sensibility. Sort of a Princess-Margaret-meets-Kate-Moss approach.

The idea that a collection is inspired by a particular person, he says, is something that happens after the fact.

> It comes at the end, to be honest, and it's often something that I don't even realise is a reference until it actually happens. I think you store things subconsciously in your mind and once I start putting the collection together and working on the shows all of a sudden I start to think, maybe there's a little touch of this person or that person.

The danger in playing around with the iconography and dress of the British is that it could easily result in a grab bag of clichés or peculiar sartorial Briticisms, but Bailey has cleverly avoided the hackneyed symbols of UK life and created a label that is, nonetheless, quintessentially British. The subtlety he brings to the design process makes his take on British dress unique. It's arguably Bailey's very Britishness that has made his strategy so successful.

The recent transformation of the 150-year-old British brand Burberry is one of the great corporate wonders of the world, and one which started a few years before Bailey was hired as the brand's creative director. In 1997 an American retailer, Rose Marie Bravo, was employed by the brand's then owners, Greater Universal Stores, to transform Burberry's of London from the purveyor of daggy raincoats into a major global luxury brand. Today Burberry produces the trend-setting or 'directional' line Burberry Prorsum, the more classic Burberry London line, and accessories and fragrances – all of which are overseen by Bailey, appointed to the role by Bravo.

Bravo was previously president of Saks Fifth Avenue and was instrumental in restoring the New York department store to its former glory. When she joined Burberry, the company had annual sales of £270 million. The label was profitable, but the brand was a mess, according to Bravo.

> It was not really a brand, in the sense that it was really just a British manufacturer of raincoats that had an international network of licensee partners . . . Each country had its own series of products that were conceived and manufactured by the local licensee. So we came in – a new team – and saw an opportunity, because when we studied the core products of Burberry and saw this truly luxurious high-quality raincoat and the factory facility, we thought, why couldn't we have all the other products commensurate with that level of detail and sophistication? We saw a niche and an opening for a British luxury goods company . . . and one that had an unbelievable receptivity in both menswear and womenswear, which is unusual.

Bravo changed the company's name from Burberry's of London to just Burberry and hired the Italian designer Roberto Menichetti to design a new Prorsum ready-to-wear range. Her initial strategy was to play on the brand's heritage. She had the iconic Burberry check incorporated into everything from ballgowns to bikinis to the paintwork on London cabs. When Bravo persuaded Kate Moss to wear the plaid bikini in one of the company's first advertising campaigns under the new management, she cut the average age of Burberry's customers by about thirty years in one fell swoop.

Bravo's success at Burberry has earned her a reputation as a corporate makeover woman, an appraisal she insists is 'over-inflated'. She prefers to see the transformation as a combination of team effort and circumstances.

We've been very fortunate to be able to attract a terrific team of people – designers, merchandisers, the creative director, our advertising and marketing team – and it's really they who should get the credit for restoring this name and transforming it into something else. [We] also had timing, because in the last ten years there has been a luxury boom and you've had everybody interested in brands. A lot of people forget that no one person is responsible for everything that happens and a lot of it has to do with what the environment is doing.

The strategy of breathing new life into the Burberry check worked, but Menichetti's Burberry Prorsum line failed to excite customers and fashion editors. In 2001, he was replaced by Bailey. By 2003, with Bravo's direction and Bailey's creative input, sales had grown to £675.8 million.

In 2004, the *New York Times* style editor, Cathy Horyn, stated:

> Menichetti managed to design clothes that had no relation to the past and, equally, no relevancy for today . . . Mr Bailey, on the other hand, correctly perceived that Burberry's history was entwined with England's.

The creative director of *GQ* magazine, Jim Moore, put it more succinctly: 'Menichetti was doing Menichetti.' Bailey, on the other hand, hit on the right balance of heritage and innovation, of Christopher Bailey and Burberry. His challenge now is to push the boundaries of what Burberry stands for.

Today Bravo is the company's vice-chairman and the company has a new CEO, Angela Ahrendts — also an American. Sales for the year ending 31 March 2007 were reported to be £850.3 million. Announcing the company's results, Ahrendts told *Women's Wear Daily* that accessories and ready-to-wear were driving the growth in sales and that outerwear — such as trench coats — accounted for 40 per cent of the business. Ahrendts also said the higher priced Prorsum line was growing.

Could it be that what Burberry needed to make it a major fashion force was American business know-how and a English sense of style? Bailey doesn't think so:

> I don't necessarily think that the creative head has to be British. I certainly think the way that I have translated the brand, it's more about the nuances as opposed to the clichés. Avoiding the clichés is always difficult, but for me it's not about the obvious references. I'm much more interested in the obscure side and subtleties of Britishness, but that's only the way that I've translated it and, happily, it's working.

Bravo, on the other hand, says it's the combination of different cultural backgrounds that has aided the success of the brand.

> Sometimes it does take someone from the outside to look at things differently. I think sometimes you can take things for granted. We've found [at Burberry] that to have more inter-cultural combinations in our management teams, a sort of melting pot of executives from different parts of the world, brings a lot of cultural interest and uniqueness if you're a global brand.

The plan has not only led to success at the cash registers but has also earned Bailey critical acclaim. In 2005 the US magazine *Forbes* called him the 'most influential designer of the year' and he was also named Designer of the Year at the British Fashion Awards.

Bailey was born in West Yorkshire — his father is a carpenter and his mother used to be the head of visual display at Marks & Spencer — and he has a typical down-to-earth Yorkshire knack for making hard work look easy and not taking it all too seriously.

> I do think it's a bit of a northern thing — we're pretty much grounded in real life. It's wonderful that you are able to meet all these incredible people and see all these incredible places, but it's not what should define you. I'm lucky to be living this kind of life. It's very hard work and demanding, but at the same time it's a privilege to be doing it.

In an interview in British *Vogue* in 2006, a friend of Bailey's, the artist Sam Taylor-Wood, said:

> He's got this extraordinary talent, yet he's also one of the most modest people I've ever met, which is an unusual attribute in his industry.

Bailey says he never dreamed of a career in fashion until his high school art teacher spotted his talent and suggested he apply to study design at Dewsbury College. He was accepted at age seventeen and from there moved to Harrow College of Art to complete a fashion degree, and then onto the Royal College of Art (RCA) to complete an MA. After graduating from the RCA he went to work for Donna Karan in New York in 1994 as the label's womenswear designer. Two years later he was snapped up by Tom Ford to be the senior womenswear designer for Gucci, a position he held until Rose Marie Bravo lured him away to be creative director of Burberry.

The high-octane, sex-fuelled, 1970s Gucci aesthetic is not exactly what you'd expect from a down-to-earth Yorkshire boy, and Bailey acknowledges the fact:

> I tried to throw myself into imagining that glamorous jet-set world of the Gucci woman, though it was a long way from my own life.

For his Burberry collections he doesn't need to stretch his imagination that far and, he says, he designs clothes he would like to wear.

Nevertheless, Bailey's Gucci training allowed him to hone his skills across all the design disciplines of a major fashion brand – from menswear to womenswear and fragrance and accessories. Magician-like, Bailey seems able to conjure up a must-have 'it' handbag – the cash cows of fashion brands – each season. To celebrate the 150th anniversary of the brand in 2006, Bailey launched the Burberry Icons collection of accessories. Orders for handbags in the Icons range, which retail for upwards of £500, jumped to 200,000 units in the year ended 31 March 2007, up from 2000 units the year before.

The starting point of each Burberry collection, says Bailey, is with colour and fabric.

I always start really with colour and the spirit of the collection. Is this season a bit more tailored or a bit more subtle, or is it more conservative? Or is this guy feeling a bit more elegant this season? Or on the other hand, is he feeling much more dishevelled and broken down, or is he more relaxed? I generally tend to think more in those terms and I start to build a colour palette really from an emotional impact I'm gravitating towards. It's an organic process whereby the collection just builds and builds – then I start doing sketches and toiles and fittings and it just grows like that. I think every day you have to be open to new inspiration.

Despite the fact that the Burberry Prorsum show notes often state what or who the inspiration behind each collection is, Bailey insists that he doesn't design to a theme each season.

I certainly think we all need something to inspire us and to aspire towards, but I don't really believe in that way of designing where you take a theme and then you work to that theme. I don't think many designers wake up in the morning and suddenly think, oh, I'm feeling *Out of Africa* today. What I try to do is to build the collections in as intelligent a way as possible and to build them so they are exciting and new and fresh, but always solidly planted in real life.

The notion of real life is something that Bailey comes back to several times in our interview.

> I love reading biographies and I love real life. I often feel that real life is much more fantastical than anything that comes from our imaginations. Real life is much more interesting than anything you could dream up.

It is a belief that informs his approach to design.

> I'm very aware of how people live their lives and what I try to do is bring out the best of people, as opposed to making people feel uncomfortable or unsure if something looks beautiful or not.

It helps that Bailey doesn't see his role at Burberry as reinventing the wheel each season. For him each collection is part of a trajectory, a continuing story, which helps explain the brand's growth. He is building on a loyal customer base. It's an approach he shares with Hedi Slimane, the former designer of Dior Homme. Slimane sees the design process as writing a new chapter in an ongoing novel each season.

Unlike Slimane, who had to create Dior Homme from a blank slate, Bailey has been fortunate in that Burberry has a rich archive for him to mine. An archive, however, can be a burden as much as an inspiration. A new collection can't be lumbered with countless references – it needs to look natural or, as Bailey would say, real. He says his role is to build on the archive.

> I don't see my role here as a static one, or just referencing what exists. I see my role as tweaking a little bit. I don't see it as revolutionising the brand, I just see it as nudging it forward always.

Having to respect the brand's heritage doesn't mean the process of working at Burberry doesn't challenge Bailey. Unlike Marc Jacobs, who says that he regards the business side of the business as a distraction and a necessary evil, Bailey thrives on the challenge of it. He has the enthusiasm of someone who has just discovered a new hobby:

> I love switching my head from going from a meeting and talking about margins and profits and then going into a meeting around colour and fabric. I don't find it boring at all, I love it. And Angela [Ahrendts] gets involved in the whole creative process as well and that's what a good professional relationship is about. It's about knowing your boundaries and knowing how involved you should be in a particular process and how comfortable you feel working with someone on something that may not be their area of expertise. You actually get inspired by them and that's the way that I see Angela. She's really my mentor and I want to learn from her.

The relationship between creative director and the CEO of the company is crucial to the success of the business, Bailey says. He worked with Ahrendts while at Donna Karan and explains:

> We know each other very well and it's essential that it's a very close relationship and that you're both singing from the same song sheet. There needs to be a creative director giving the brand the image and the vision for the company on an aesthetic level, and then you need a business person who has the vision for the business part of the company. And those people need to be completely in sync.

Despite his and Burberry's success, Bailey doesn't really see himself as a power broker in the fashion industry.

> I still see myself as the new kid and probably always will. I still have my school friends I grew up with and I'm very grounded in real life. There are really two sides to me. When I'm working, which is pretty much all the time, I'm very crazed and I do live a very hectic life and it's very demanding and very challenging. And then I do have this other part of my life that is extremely serene and goes very much back to my roots. Again, I do think it's a bit of a northern thing.

SUNJOO MOON

An interview with Sunjoo Moon is never brief. My first tape rolls on as we chat about nothing in particular. Australian-raised but Paris-based, Moon wants to know what the weather is like in Sydney at the moment, what's happening in the fashion scene, which designers are hot right now and which stores are stocking the best labels, what restaurants to go to, what the current situation with property prices is. Another tape goes into the recorder.

As well as being a great conversationalist, Moon is a master storyteller, and with her family connections she has great fodder for a good yarn. Whereas Sunjoo Moon headed to Paris after high school to work in the fashion industry, her sister Unjoo studied filmmaking and found her way to the centre of the movie world, Los Angeles. Unjoo is married to the Australian cinematographer Dion Beebe, whom she met while at film school. Beebe was the director of photography on *Memoirs of a Geisha* and received an Academy Award for his work on the film. So Sunjoo Moon can't help herself and is itching to tell a fellow Australian a funny story about something that happened at the award ceremony.

Unjoo had invited her Sydney-based father to attend, along with Beebe's mother. At the *Vanity Fair* Oscar party after the awards, Beebe asked his father-in-law to hold his gold statuette while he and his wife headed to the dance floor. No sooner did this happen than the flashbulbs started going off around Mr Moon. Naturally enough he reasoned that perhaps people just wanted a photo of someone with an Oscar – any someone and any Oscar. It wasn't until two men approached him and told him how much his film meant to them that Mr Moon realised he was being mistaken for Ang Lee, the director of the Academy Award–winning film *Brokeback Mountain,* who had also won an Oscar that evening.

When Mr Moon told his daughter and son-in-law what had happened they were standing with the actor Jamie Foxx, who had worked with Beebe on the films *Collateral* and *Miami Vice.* Unjoo said they'd all had a good laugh at the case of mistaken identity and Foxx told them that white Americans always think that people who aren't white all look the same. The fact that Lee is from Taiwan and the Moons are from Korea would be too subtle a point for the Oscar-struck paparazzi.

The concept of national identity is a difficult one for Sunjoo Moon. She was born in Korea, raised in Australia and has lived in Paris for almost two decades. She also did a stint in Italy, and her young children speak several languages. She prefers to see herself as a global citizen, but one who still calls Australia home. When she shows off her newly renovated apartment in Paris she makes a point of demonstrating the Australian-designed and manufactured light switches. It's all so terribly chic and cosmopolitan.

For fashion designers, being 'international' often just means they have boutiques in several countries. It rarely has anything to do with the designer's handwriting (distinctive style) or their approach to the fashion industry. International, however, is an adjective that Sunjoo Moon likes to use quite a bit in conversation.

Her sister Unjoo is equally international in her outlook. Between films, Unjoo Moon runs a fashion boutique on Melrose Avenue in Los Angeles called Sheila. The boutique stocks only Australian and New Zealand designers. Somehow that extends to stocking her sister Sunjoo's collections.

Because of her background, people — fashion critics, wholesale buyers, retail customers — find it difficult to pigeonhole Sunjoo Moon. In Australian stores she's not thought of as an Australian designer, nor is she considered an international label. Nevertheless she is regarded as one of Australia's most successful expatriate fashion designers.

Moon grew up in the Sydney suburb of Gordon, and after finishing high school she left Australia in 1985 to attend the famed Studio Berçot design school, traditionally a training ground for designers with an ambition to work in haute couture. After graduating from Studio Berçot in 1987, Moon became a rising star of the international fashion industry, designing for prestigious brands such as Missoni, Cerruti and Thierry Mugler.

Moon's biggest success came when she was hired as the head designer of womenswear at Missoni and was charged with revamping the staid Italian brand. Her strategy was to go back to what made the Missoni label famous in the first place: its complex geometric prints and knitwear. Moon reinterpreted the signature prints in new fabrics and colours and created a ready-to-wear collection around them that was an instant sensation. After her first collection for Missoni hit the catwalks — winter 1996/97 — *Women's Wear Daily* declared: 'The 42-year-old fashion house is back in force.' Her success at Missoni earned her a reputation as a Ms Fix-It — a designer capable of breathing new life into old brands. In 2005 she launched her first collection under her own name and, in a strange twist for someone who has spent so long working in the world's fashion capitals, chose Sydney as the place to launch the label.

Sunjoo Moon's show at Australian Fashion Week in 2006 was one of the most hotly anticipated catwalk debuts in the nine-year-old

event's history. Only it wasn't really a debut. All of which meant expectations were almost impossibly high.

> I wanted to come up with something of my own, my own personal point of view. I wanted it to be my expression and for it to be in my own name. I've spent all my time developing businesses and making money for other people and now I really wanted to structure myself and make my own business and create an international label with my name. My whole game is to structure and build an international label, because I don't think that any label can survive by just being national.
>
> Because of my cultural background, having been born in Asia and grown up in Australia and living in France, my feeling is that what I do and my design approach is actually quite international – I really can't think of another word for it. I have a name which is fundamentally Asian, but my style is definitely not Asian. It's also not Australian and it's not French. It's kind of a mishmash.

Moon chose Sydney to launch her new brand because the decision to go out on her own was such a personal one, and so the best place to do it was on her home turf.

> Sydney is a really personal and sentimental place for me because it's where I grew up and in a way it's still home. And also because I've

always had a lot of support here. It's not that I don't have support in Europe, it's just that I don't want to do a show in Paris until I have a lot of money behind me, because there's really no point. You're just one of the hundreds of shows done on a shoestring budget and you're up against the big, big players who think nothing of spending €2 million on a collection show. I wanted my show in Sydney to be more low profile, but I definitely didn't want people to think, 'Oh, she's from Paris, she's here to show us how to do it.'

She needn't have worried. Within seconds of the lights going up at the end of the parade, it was clear that the homecoming queen had delivered. It was one of the few times that Colette Garnsey, the general manager of fashion at Australia's premier department store, David Jones, was spotted jumping to her feet and making for the talent at the finale. Indeed, it was business cards at twenty paces, as buyers from David Jones and its main rival Myer vied for Moon's attention.

Garnsey said of the parade:

It was a standout of Australian Fashion Week. The things that struck me first of all were the original fabrics and prints and the impeccable tailoring — it stood out throughout the entire collection. To see that level of finish in the garments is, I think, a reflection of her international experience.

Moon's international focus serves a useful purpose for David Jones too, though Garnsey finds it difficult to pigeonhole the label as simply 'international'.

> It's hard to classify in that way. I see it as a fabulous bridge between our portfolio of international brands and our Australian brands. It will fit between collections like Burberry, Paul Smith and Moschino.

Although Moon was almost bewildered by the attention, it was a satisfying moment:

> Despite all my theories and justifications around showing my debut collection in Australia, I wasn't exactly all that prepared. I didn't even show the entire collection. I just flew out to Australia a couple of days before the show with two suitcases of clothing. My attitude was to just put on the show and to have a bit of fun really. I giggled throughout the entire show . . . it was an easy and very relaxed atmosphere. It's so different to showing in Paris. The buyers and the press in Paris are under obligation to see all the big name shows so unless you put on a consequential show it's hard to stand out. Compared to AFW it's just so stressful and I don't know how much a small brand actually gets out of it. AFW on the other hand is all nice and friendly. You do things like go out for a drink after the show and it has a nice and easy pace.

Depending on your point of view, Moon's career path has either been sensible (first honing her craft at big companies that offered guidance and security) or self-effacing (preferring to stay in the shadows and design under someone else's name). Whichever way you choose to look at it, however, she appears to have put those days behind her.

> The decision to go out on my own was also a product of the fact that I now feel ready to do it. I've been though a lot of things in my personal life and gained a lot of experience in my professional life and now I feel ready to do it. Maybe I just wasn't ready before. When you're working for a big company you feel protected in a way.

Nevertheless, it was a gamble, and some parts of the fashion industry were understandably reluctant to let her make that transition. Moon says she has been contacted recently by quite a few companies looking for a designer.

> They're really big, well-known names, and it's kind of natural for them to gravitate towards me because they know I do revamps of big names. But that's exactly what I'm trying not to do now.

Although Moon does consult for some companies on a freelance basis, the bulk of her time is now devoted to her own label.

I just go in half a day a week and give them [the other brands] directions on colours, what they should be doing, change their shapes, do some fittings for them, but I don't have to overhaul the whole thing. It's a great situation because I can do things anonymously as my name is not attached to the label.

Moon first attempted to create her own label two years earlier, while she was head designer at Thierry Mugler, but found her day job got in the way.

Basically when I tried to launch my own label in 2004 I was spending 90 per cent of my time directing a design team in a big company and only 10 per cent of my time on my own collection, and it suffered because of it. Now I spend 90 per cent of my time on my own collection and 10 per cent working for other people.

In 2006 Moon decided to take the plunge and accept investment from a business partner to allow her to expand. Moon joined forces with Sterling International, a leading Paris-based recruitment and consulting firm for the fashion industry. The move has allowed her to open a sales and public relations office in New York to tap into the potentially lucrative US market. Moon resisted the idea of a financial backer at first, but says she came around because it was the right offer at the right time.

It's like a marriage. You have to feel right about it if it's going to be a good marriage. It's all about how the two parties fit together. Personally, I think I resisted it when I had offers of financial backing before because, frankly, I'm too much of a control freak.

The financial backing has enabled Moon not only to widen her distribution, but also to expand into accessories such as shoes and handbags and to start a second, more affordable, diffusion line.

A second line would keep my first line very up-market and my second line would then be more of a separates collection. But it won't be casual, because I don't really do casual.

Indeed she doesn't: despite the use of colour in her collections, Moon's own personal style tends towards the monochromatic and in particular black. She gives the impression of effortless chic in the way that only French women can, a natural by-product of her life in Paris.

Moon certainly learned a great deal from the houses for which she has worked. One of the more striking elements of her first collection was its coherence — the entire collection centred on a theme of circles and spots.

My initial thought was, 'What do you want to see in stores after winter?' And my reaction to that was, 'Everyone likes a spot.' It just keeps on going from there, and the collection was about creating a story around spots. From the spot I thought, okay, anything I do with this collection has to take the idea further. So that went into designing jacquard spots and doing spots on prints, or several prints of spots together on the same dress. Then from that I had circle pockets on dresses. It just keeps going and going. It was about creating a story around spots and then just developing it.

And, in any collection I do, there's always purple. There's something about purple that I find is really strong. It's really feminine. There's a particular purple I love as well, the purple that leans more towards the fuschia than the blue. In one way or another I always have something in my collection in purple — it's just one of those things. My shopfront is purple too.

The other notable feature of that first collection was the outstanding quality of Moon's fabrics and manufacturing. It's a quality and refinement in tailoring normally associated with luxury brands that carry a much higher price tag. And quality tailoring is not a feat many designers producing relatively small collections can pull off.

Maybe the thing I learned the most from my time with [the big fashion houses] is a certain level of perfectionism in manufacturing. I also developed relationships with the best fabric manufacturers in Europe and I've continued that relationship with my own line.

The fabrics used in Moon's collection are all exclusive to her and the range is manufactured in France.

> It's very difficult to get the manufacturers to do small series of prints; they all want to do only big runs. But, with these manufacturers, I've made huge business for them working for big companies, so they know me and I'm able to do smaller series.

As well as making important contacts with suppliers and manufacturers during her time with the big fashion houses, Moon also learned about some of the more mundane, but not less helpful, aspects of the fashion industry.

> One of the best lessons I had was about the importance of structuring your business to deliver on time. For example, we deliver to our retailers in December, whereas most people deliver in late January. I think it's a good way to establish a business by delivering early and earning a reputation for being reliable.

Moon's approach to designing clothes is also highly practical.

> You want to look a certain way and you want to be perceived in a certain way. Clothes are the way you project yourself to the outside world. Sometimes you don't want a garment that's wacky and has three sleeves or something. There's a certain reality [about

my designs], maybe because that's also my personality. I'm a very realistic person.

It's an attitude that's appreciated by her fans. 'As a non-twenty-something, hers were clothes I could absolutely imagine myself wearing — and will wear,' says Kirsty Cameron, formerly the editor-in-chief of *InStyle* Australia and now editorial director of women's lifestyle titles for ACP Magazines in New Zealand.

Moon also understands where she fits into the broader fashion industry:

> I have this great belief that fashion today has gone to two extremes: either you're at the very high, ultra-luxury end or you are in the mass market. At one end, you've got luxury fashion, which is very high quality and usually associated with a name, and at the other end you've got the mass market, where you've got pretty much the same look, same fabric, at one-tenth the price. There's no middle market any more.

She explains that with the cost of fabric determined by the quantity ordered, companies such as the massive Spanish clothing chain Zara are able to buy the same quality as high-end designers, but at a fraction of the price.

> Zara buy fabrics of the same quality as the designer collections . . . they're buying it in lots of 50,000 metres, so the price comes down.

This, combined with the fact that they take inspiration from the catwalks and have short lead times, is killing the luxury fashion industry, according to Moon:

> As a designer now, you've got to understand the market and the times we are living in. The only way to exist now is to come in with a very strong identity, there's not even any point in trying to compete on price. There's almost no point in a designer doing basics any more, because customers will just go to Zara [for that]. My conviction is that clothes have to be beautifully made and with beautiful fabrics, or else why would women want to buy them?

The 1990s concept of the head-to-toe designer look is, Moon says, no longer something women aspire to.

> I think women who have money now, they don't want to look like they are wearing a 'label'. What luxury is now is to have something that other people don't and to create your own style. I think consumers have become very smart. I think the consumer doesn't want to look as if she is wearing one label from head-to-toe with matching shoes and a bag all from the same collection. I think she wants to look as though she has her own personality and individuality. She wants to wear things that are beautiful and beautifully made. She knows when she's getting her money's worth and the product has to stand up on its own no matter who you are.

# ENNIO CAPASA

## COSTUME NATIONAL

E nnio Capasa, the Italian designer of the modernist and minimalist label Costume National, is a connoisseur of vintage clothing. He traces his passion for the pre-worn back to when he was a teenager, long before our present-day fad for all things old, and describes himself as 'an addict'. Capasa estimates he owns more than 10,000 pieces of vintage clothing – men's and women's – that he has collected over the years, mostly from flea markets. Some pieces he buys to wear, others he just admires.

> Sometimes I buy a beautiful piece just because I love it . . . sometimes
> I can't use it because it's not practical, or it's not the right time.

Capasa says his obsession with the beauty of the clothed human body is a consequence of being Italian:

> It's part of our nationality, the Italian obsession with looking good,

with beauty. Italian people are surrounded by beauty, in a way, which is what, I think, makes us great producers of beauty.

Capasa founded Costume National in 1986 with his brother Carlo, and showed his first women's collection in 1987, but success did not come overnight.

> We couldn't get anyone to come to our shows. We first showed in a beautiful old space, L'Umanitaria in Milan, which is a wonderful room and with designs by Leonardo da Vinci. We even had live musicians and still only about thirty people came to our show. In those days designers such as Giorgio Armani and Gianni Versace had the Milan scene sewn up and it was very hard for new designers to get attention.

The breakthrough came in the early 1990s, when Capasa started to find that good vintage clothing was harder and harder to come by. It was becoming especially difficult for him to find clothes he wanted to wear. So he did what any self-respecting fashion designer would do: he started a menswear business.

It was only then, after the debut of Costume National Homme in 1993, that the label drew the attention of fashion journalists. One of the first people to champion Capasa's talents was the influential *New York Times* fashion critic, the late Amy Spindler. Just a few years later, she would declare Capasa to be one of the most influential designers of the 1990s, praising him for redefining how men dress, changing the silhouette of men's tailoring and altering the overall perception of men's fashion.

Like his appreciation of vintage clothing, Capasa's approach to menswear is, in some respects, a by-product of his very Italianness. 'Growing up I was the kind of boy that was comfortable wearing classic tailoring,' Capasa says, as nonchalantly as an Australian male might admit to being comfortable in shorts, T-shirt and thongs.

> It's an Italian way of dressing, because we have a strong link with tailoring. In every small city and village there is always a church and there is always a tailor – it's an essential part of every city and small village. The diffusion of that sensibility was gigantic and it meant that Italy doesn't really have the same sense of sportswear as Americans do, for example.

Perhaps as a result of this heritage, Capasa doesn't see the men's universe as divided into the usual categories of work and play, day and night, formal and casual. He designs clothes for men who want to look good at any time and he sees suiting as an essential part of his 'vision of how to be elegant' on any occasion.

> If you look at every collection I do, there is always the suit. I really think it's something that men enjoy wearing. When I first introduced

my men's suits I had the strongest feeling that what I wanted to do was to change the traditional silhouette. To make it more sexy, but at the same time to make it even more tailored. I just can't think of Costume National without thinking about suits.

On the day we met he wore a suit jacket with denim jeans, a T-shirt and cravat. With his mop of black curly hair and pencil-thin moustache, this outfit made him look like a cartoon character of an Italian fashion designer. He told me that he had loved fashion from an early age. 'Ever since I was thirteen or fourteen I had a love of fashion and I wanted to dress in a way that felt sexy.'

The Capasa brothers were born in the baroque town of Lecce, in Puglia, southern Italy (the heel part of the boot); the children, not surprisingly, of tailors.

The family was quite wealthy and had several clothing stores, including the hip boutique 'Smart', which had its heyday in the 1950s. Ennio, who was born in 1960, took an interest in the business right from the start.

I lived my infancy between Mary Quant and Yves Saint Laurent, going on trips with my folks to London as a teenager. I was born a very good consumer. My main interest was to buy beautiful things, not to design them. That feeling was very strong in me until I was about sixteen or seventeen and then I became a punk.

In his late teens Capasa travelled throughout Japan and developed an interest in Zen and the writings of Yukio Mishima. On his return to Italy he was accepted into the sculpture course at the Brera Academy of Fine Arts in Milan. (His interest in contemporary art has remained strong and he is a respected figure in the Italian contemporary arts scene.) Then, at the age of about twenty-two, he got back into fashion again. 'Eventually *la moda* brought me back. My family was born in fashion and my parents were both *molto* trendy.'

After Capasa graduated from art school, a friend sent some of his fashion illustrations to the Japanese designer Yohji Yamamoto. Impressed with the talent he saw in the drawings, Yamamoto invited Capasa to work for him in his studio in Tokyo. It was a job he held for almost three years and one that would have a profound effect on his design philosophy.

His brother Carlo also spent the early part of his fashion career honing his craft inside a big company. Carlo Capasa worked alongside the Italian designer Romeo Gigli and then, later, as a consultant to the creative director of Gucci, Dawn Mello.

When the Capasas eventually set up their own label, Ennio chose the name 'Costume National' because, frankly, he liked the sound of it.

It's true that it doesn't make sense when you look at it from the outside. But when I started the business I was young and I don't know why, but I didn't want to use my own name. I wanted to do something more mysterious. A project where nobody knew who was behind it. And I never used to do interviews or anything like that.

It is a name that means everything and nothing, equally plausible and equally foreign in French, English or Italian. And it has layers of irony. It sounds utilitarian and practical – a good name for a Soviet suit maker perhaps – and yet that simplicity is actually rather complex. Yamamoto's influence is apparent in Capasa's design handwriting; perhaps the name of his company could be read as a piece of playful 'Japlish', a continuation of the enigma that another Japanese designer, Rei Kawakubo, created when she gave her label, Comme des Garçons, a very ambiguous and ironic French-sounding name.

A significant part of Costume National's aesthetic directly derives from Capasa's exposure to the Japanese obsession with fabric technology, which he has artfully combined with the artisanal traditions of Italian tailoring. His suits at Costume National make use of techno fabrics such as nylons – so beloved of Japanese designers – rather than wool, a fabric that Italy has a long and proud history of manufacturing.

This Japanese influence, which set Capasa apart from his fellow Italian designers right from the start, also led him to abandon Milan in favour of Paris. In the early 1980s the organisers of the Milan fashion shows had repeatedly refused requests by Japanese designers such as Yamamoto and Kawakubo, so they looked instead to Paris to launch themselves onto the international market. In 1991 Capasa decided to follow their lead and show in the French capital, where he found the respect of critics and his peers in the industry, finally overcoming the poor reaction to his designs on his home turf.

At this point he realised that 'people needed to see who was behind the label'. Capasa says it was Amy Spindler who urged him to come out of the shadows, when she wrote in *The New York Times* that if you're a serious fashion designer you must take responsibility and show your face. 'So now I think that everyone knows that Costume National and Ennio Capasa are the same thing,' he says.

And yet, despite Capasa's Japanese influences, his label's nonsensical, French-sounding name, and his annual shows in Paris, Costume National could not be more Italian.

Based in Milan, it is wholly owned and operated by the two brothers. Ennio is president of the company and responsible for the design of the collections, while CEO Carlo takes care of the business side of things. Even the way the Capasas run their business, Ennio says, is quintessentially Italian. It started small, as a family company. It wasn't until 1996 that the brand opened its first stores in Milan and Tokyo (soon after came Los Angeles and New York). Today there are ten Costume National boutiques and several 'concept' stores in department stores globally. The company became vertically integrated when it bought its own factory in 1998. ('Vertical integration' is owning all the steps in the chain: manufacturing, distribution and retail.) It recently added a factory for shoes in Padua, another apparel plant in Vicenza and a leather treatment company in Lecce. Capasa explains:

> It's a company that has, more or less, about three hundred people on the payroll and we have a structure and management in place to grow the business, but still my brother and I have a lot of control. So in other words this is a family company with control of every situation. In Italy most companies are born like that and then they might become something else. It's very typical to have this kind of relationship, it's part of our culture.

Even though fashion brands — no matter how critically acclaimed — need huge amounts of cash to be able to expand globally, the ownership of Italian companies such as Giorgio Armani, Versace and Dolce & Gabbana has typically remained with the creators of those brands. Giorgio Armani, for example, is the solitary shareholder of his fashion empire.

In the past ten years, however, business culture has been rocked and Italian businesses have not been exempt from the consequences. In the early 1990s, large conglomerates snaffled up smaller fashion brands with untapped potential. Casualties included Bottega Veneta and Sergio Rossi (now part of the French-controlled Gucci group), and Fendi, once entirely family owned but now owned by LVMH. The money the big companies offer is substantial, which makes the pressure to sell intense.

Capasa says that in 2000 he was approached by 'a major company' — although he won't say which one.

I thought about it for a couple of weeks and decided not to sell, which maybe was a big mistake because the money at the time was enormous. This is part of what it's like to be independent. The pressure to sell was strong and it was like fighting with a knife against an atomic bomb. It was an interesting challenge and in the end I think I was right, because if you look at people like Helmut Lang and Jil Sander, they both resigned from their companies [after their labels were acquired by Prada]. Look at Alexander McQueen: it lost 15 million euros [in 2004]. Balenciaga, 12 million, Stella McCartney, 10 million. [Alexander McQueen, Balenciaga and Stella McCartney are all owned by Gucci.] So it says to me that it's very difficult for an independent designer to work in that kind of system because it doesn't really work if you think how much money is lost. We are one of the few fashion houses that actually grew in the early 2000s in the face of the incredible power of the conglomerates.

The luxury goods system doesn't work, says Capasa: so much money must be pumped into a brand in order for it to realise its expansion plans that a return on investment can be a long way off, and the parent company grows nervous.

As well as the financial pressure of belonging to a conglomerate, Capasa says, there's the issue of the brand's 'authenticity'. In a *New Yorker* magazine profile on the designer Helmut Lang published in 2000 – shortly after Lang's label was acquired by Prada – Capasa said he did not see how a serious designer could sell to a company such as Prada and maintain his or her independence and creative freedom and at the same time stay authentic. 'And if you are no longer authentic, what is the point?' he asked.

Capasa explains what he means by authentic: 'One vision, one style, one point of view,' he says.

> Today the fashion business is overcrowded and there is too much marketing, so valuing the authenticity of a brand is one of the most important things you need. Of course you need a strong manager and a good organisation around you. But without authenticity . . . what do you have?

Capasa believes absolutely in his own label's authenticity: 'There is no distinction between who I am and what I do.'

Sales started to plateau in 2001; since then Capasa has pushed

Costume National into new frontiers. The company entered into a licensing agreement with the Italian company Marcolin to produce a line of sunglasses. And to generate even more revenue, Costume National launched a signature fragrance in collaboration with the Japanese cosmetics company Kanebo in 2002. In keeping with the company's minimalist style its first scent was called, simply, 'Scent'. Capasa deliberately chose a roller ball design like a deodorant:

> When I used to go out with a large gang of people someone would always spray a shot of scent in the taxi, which I detested. I was always too embarrassed to say anything, but I promised myself that if I ever made a perfume I would make it a roll-on.

Recently Capasa decided to do something that sounds very 1990s but is in fact, he says, part of an Italian tradition in fashion: he started a diffusion line.

> If you look at the history of Italian fashion it's a model that is excellent for the growth of the business. If you look, for example, at a traditional Italian house like Giorgio Armani, when he made the diffusion line [Emporio Armani, Armani Jeans, Armani Exchange] it was a very big step and it was very important for his career. Recently Dolce & Gabbana have done the same thing with the D&G line.

In 2004 Costume National launched the C'N'C label, a streetwear line for men and women manufactured and distributed under licence by the Italian company Ittierre.

The strategy with C'N'C was to take the company in two different directions. Costume National would stay much more high end and C'N'C would be kept as a streetwear label and be sold in more outlets than the main line. It's possible to have two different lines that exist together but grow in different directions, very much like the DKNY model [Donna Karan's diffusion line]. The diffusion line is something that is sold in much greater volumes. So it makes the brand much more widely known. If it's a good diffusion brand, one that is original, then it can be a good generator of cash.

According to Capasa the first year sales of C'N'C were 140 per cent above expectations – but given the designer's feelings about brand authenticity, might not C'N'C be considered a risky venture?

From my point of view every new project you do is a risk. At the same time I think that risk helps you to grow, because you have the responsibility of having your own money invested in the company. If you don't [take on] risk by yourself then you can never really have a strong, focused vision. If you analyse the real Dior or the real Saint Laurent, for example, they were involved with their own money in the company and for me, as a designer, it's very important. Fashion is an industry. It's an artistic industry, a creative industry, but it's still an industry and so I think the relationship between designer and finances is important for understanding that.

This pragmatism is symptomatic of Capasa's approach to fashion design. His mantra, he says, is to make real clothes that can be adopted into a customer's wardrobe, rather than dictating new trends each season. It's a utilitarian philosophy that could have seen Capasa consigned to the ranks of a mere clothing manufacturer – if it wasn't for his sophisticated marriage of sleek ready-to-wear with the Italian sartorial tradition.

For spring/summer 2006 the C'N'C label launched an additional collection in collaboration with the Italian motorcycle company Ducati. The collection, called C'N'C Ducati, is sold in 200 exclusive boutiques worldwide. There are also plans to open a monobrand store in Milan. C'N'C Ducati will reinvent the concept of the urban biker, says Capasa, mixing it with traditional Italian aesthetics. The line includes jeans, bags, leather bomber jackets, limited edition T-shirts and trainers – priced 20 to 30 per cent below the main Costume National line.

The Ducati venture may very well be a marriage made in fashion heaven. Italians love their motorbikes and scooters nearly as much as they love their clothes. Capasa has even designed a Costume National special edition Ducati motorbike. The partnership is just one more example of Capasa's blending together of style and culture and of his business being influenced by his life and his passions.

JOSH GOOT

In 1995, Isaac Mizrahi was huge. He was showered in accolades: his talent was bigger, his clothes better and more beautiful than anything that had preceded them, and he was the subject of the major documentary film *Unzipped*. Just a few years later, Mizrahi was out of business – the fashion industry is nothing if not fickle.

Today, though, Isaac Mizrahi is bigger than ever. He had a most improbable saviour – the discount department store Target. That a store like Target should employ a designer of Mizrahi's calibre was unthinkable at the time. It turns out, however, that he was a trailblazer. Target is now making a name for itself as the store that brings good design to the masses through its 'Designers for Target' program, thanks in no small part to the success of the range that Mizrahi designs for the US Target chain.

In Australia in 2006 Target commissioned fashion ranges from local designers including Tina Kalivas, Alice McCall and T.L. Wood. In early 2007 the department store released a range by the British designer Stella McCartney and caused frenzied scenes as women clamoured to buy designs bearing McCartney's name at around one-tenth of the price of her main line, backed by French luxury conglomerate PPR.

In May 2007 the store announced that Josh Goot would be the next designer to take part in Target's program, creating a limited range of budget-priced cutting-edge fashion. Goot was reportedly paid $100,000 to design the range — a far cry from McCartney's reported $1 million, but the cash will no doubt prove helpful as Goot attempts to make his label a major global brand. Being stocked by a store like Target would once have been the kiss of death for a fashion designer, the end of the road. Today it's the ultimate honour and a springboard to success.

Josh Goot is that rarest of fashion designers: a 'next big thing' who has the stuff to actually make it big. He launched his eponymous fashion label at Australian Fashion Week in 2005 when he was just twenty-five years old. Since then he has garnered critical acclaim at home and launched his business on the international market, where he also received high praise, making the cover of the American fashion bible, *Women's Wear Daily*. Goot's debut show in 2005 was a much-needed wake-up call in an otherwise dreary Australian Fashion Week.

It's definitely a cliché to say that covering a fashion week as a journalist is like running a marathon, but as clichés go it's an apt one. Shows start at 9 am and sometimes run through until as late as 10 pm, often without time for life's necessities, such as eating. In just one week you see more than 100 shows: some good, some bad, but, if you're lucky, one or two of them will be extraordinary. Unfortunately you have to sit through the dross to find the gems. No journalist wants to skip a show they think might be bad, just in case the designer becomes the next big thing – the Holy Grail of any fashion season. Fashion is, after all, about the discovery of the new. Four days into the week, Goot's show was that discovery: an extraordinary new designer.

Goot's approach to fashion is so disarmingly simple that after his debut show many commentators declared it to be 'futuristic', due mainly, perhaps, to the prevalence of silvery fabric in the collection. Goot's version of the future, however, is more about small increments of change than giant leaps forward each season. His first collection was less a shock to the system than a reminder of what fashion is all about – which means he has also been called a 'classicist'. 'I think that fashion should be easy and that clothes should be comfortable,' he says. 'Basically this brand is about tailored comfort.'

For his first collection Goot showed a range of men's and women's clothing made entirely from cotton jersey – or T-shirt material – which included such items as blazers, trench coats and trousers.

They were precisely cut and beautifully finished, in cool blues, whites and muted silver. Goot has further explored his notion of tailored comfort in subsequent collections and introduced lightweight wool jersey into the mix for winter, which makes for a slouchy new take on the traditional men's suit – less structured and more casual.

In his spring/summer 2008 collection, he took the idea one step further and sought inspiration, he says, from Ancient Rome. Goot showed in this collection that he isn't afraid to experiment and again introduced new fabrics – blends, he says, 'that perform at a higher level'. Garments made from superfine grey marl viscose stood out, as did a series of singlets and leggings made from the sheerest polyamide acrylic in silver and gold. After the all-black collection he had shown for winter in New York just a few weeks earlier, Goot put on a display of colour for summer. There were acid yellows, hot pinks and body-hugging dresses in blocks of solid colour, as well as some very chic cocktail frocks.

> Those signature things – the trench coats, the dresses, the singlets, et cetera – are kind of the foundation of the collection and have been tweaked each season and I suppose gradually perfected. The label is more about an evolution than an inspiration or a brand new theme for each season.

Goot describes the aesthetic of his label as 'a return to clean . . . simple but still fully finished.'

My design process is more about taking things out than putting things in. There are a million things you can do and that's the easy part. The hard part is paring it back, paring it back, paring it back.

It's important for a collection to have some type of neutral foundation. We've always used the grey marl as one of our signature shades because we felt that from the outset it helped capture our foundation message, which was the idea of T-shirting in tailored pieces. To me the grey marl is that typical T-shirt kind of fabric. We still really believe in that concept and that's why the grey marl is still there. This season the colour might be the same but the way we're dealing with the grey marl is completely different. It's evolved from the way we originally used it, which was in 100 per cent cotton, to now where we are using it in 100 per cent viscose.

In a certain way Goot's decision to design a range for Target makes perfect sense: his clothes, while not to deny their technical aspect, are not exactly about luxury fabrics. There's no leather, crocodile, cashmere or fur here. His clothes are not exactly priced at the luxury level either. All of which makes for the perfect transition from up-market boutiques to Target, but therein lies the rub. A trench coat from Stella McCartney's main line could be made in a luxurious fabric such as silk and retail for about $3000; one from Josh Goot is substantially less at around the $800 mark, and possibly made in a mundane fabric such as cotton. So while McCartney's work for Target delivers her designs to a market that would otherwise not consider buying them – the Target McCartney trench coat was $250 – Goot is straying into a grey area where he might just compromise his main business.

At the top end of the industry, clothing is often handmade from luxurious fabrics in one-of-a-kind designs, and carries very high price tags. At the other end there is mass-market clothing, produced in factories outside the country of origin of the designer, carrying very affordable price tags and looking remarkably similar to the high-end product. And in the middle, you have a bunch of designers struggling to find their relevance.

What will save Goot from compromising his main line with his collection for Target is his relevance in the middle market. As Goot says:

> The brand is about filling voids and plugging into the market and trying to cater for an element of the market that's not necessarily being catered for. We're not trying to be a complete designer brand and we're also not trying to be a contemporary brand; we're just trying to plug in between the two.

Generally what is happening in fashion now is kind of reflective of certain movements in society – everything needs to be a little more accessible and easier and that's what we are trying to reflect in the clothes. Clean ease is what we are trying to capture. I think it's great that Target give a wider audience access to great clothes and great designs. It's one of the more exciting initiatives or developments in global fashion this millennium.

Goot may appear to have the golden touch, with his young label already being stocked in prestigious stores such as Neiman Marcus and Henri Bendel in the US and Colette in Paris, but his relatively short career in fashion has not been without its bumps. Before designing under his own name, Goot launched the streetwear label Platform in 2004, which failed due to a mix of youth and inexperience. He admits it was a case of learning the hard way.

The two years since he launched the label bearing his own name have been a fast ride for Goot. When he showed his spring/summer 2008 collection at Australian Fashion Week in May 2007 it was his fourth runway show in twelve months. He'd returned to Sydney in March after showing in New York in February and put together a collection in just six weeks.

Goot is typical of a growing trend among the Australian fashion fraternity to get launched and get out. By chance, invitation or grit,

Australian fashion designers are making it where it matters – beyond the claustrophobically small Australian market. 'The future of the label rests overseas,' says Goot.

> That's not to understate the importance of the Australian market – it's still important and is currently our biggest market. But in order to really grow the brand we have to look overseas as the place to do that.

It's a sentiment that a growing number of Australian designers seem to share. In the last few years Kit Willow, Jayson Brunsdon, Ksubi (formerly Tsubi), Toni Maticevski and Sass & Bide have all taken their wares to New York Fashion Week. They chose New York over, say, Paris, because it is seen as the place to do business. Paris is where you go if you're a great artist; London is often the launching pad to Paris; but New York is where you go if you want to get into American department stores, which means it's the international marketplace you go to if you're at the more commercial end of fashion.

For Goot, though, the decision to show in New York was as personal as it was professional:

> The general aesthetic of our label has a relevance in America because of its ease and simplicity. I suppose the sportswear essence in the label is also quite American.

Goot is not simply hell-bent on growth for growth's sake. Before he made the decision to show his collections in New York he did quite a bit of market research and soul searching.

> I went to New York in early 2006 just to get a sense of it and to see where we fit in the American market and in the global context. Is there a place for us in the market? Are we offering something different? Can we compete with these people? And the answer I came to about all those questions is yes.

Goot has received high praise for his unique take on fashion, but there are many critics who question whether he has the talent to stay the course. After his first show in New York in September 2006, Style.com's Nicole Phelps gave his show a lukewarm review and said:

> . . . to make it here, or more precisely on the runway, he'll have to develop a more pointed design message, and leave the primary colors down under.

Goot takes the reaction in his stride and sees it as more of a challenge than a discouragement. Like so many things that appear to be simple, sometimes it just takes a while for people to get his style.

> We have received a degree of attention in Australia and we have been able to define the label there quite effectively. In America a lot of

people get it and a lot of people don't, which to me is actually very promising. I kind of prefer that some people don't get it, whether they are retailers or media or whatever.

Some American retailers simply don't know how to pigeonhole his label, because unlike many young designers, he is not trying to be all things to all people.

> American retailers are like, where does it fit within the context of my store, because it's T-shirting, but it's tailored, and sure it's styled real slick, but it's a T-shirt basically and I just don't really see where it goes.

Nevertheless, Goot remains adamant that the US is the best potential export market for his label because of its origins in sportswear. 'It suits the American way of life more so than a European one,' he says. The sportswear influence, the minimalism and the almost utilitarian approach to clothing in Goot's collections have invited comparisons to Helmut Lang. Goot's design approach is more than just minimalism for the sake of it and, like Lang before him, he has an instinct for the appeal of basic items like T-shirts. Josh Goot has created a whole new field of luxury fashion.

ADAM LIPPES

Sitting in the bottom drawer of my wardrobe is a navy blue T-shirt purchased in New York in 1992. I have been wearing the T-shirt for fifteen years and despite the fact that the collar is starting to come away from the fabric and there are a few growing holes under the arms I have no intention of throwing it out in the foreseeable future. It's a brand of no particular consequence and holds no real sentimental value. Not to mention that after fifteen years of washing it's not even a particularly nice colour anymore. I've kept it all this time, when far more expensive T-shirts have come and gone in my closet, because it fits just right: it's not too tight or too baggy, the sleeves are just the right length and the fabric is the softest cotton. It is the perfect T-shirt. If I could find this T-shirt in a store today I would buy a lifetime's supply of them.

In fashion terms, the quest for the perfect white T-shirt is so enduring it could almost be biblical; one reason perhaps why it took a man called Adam to finally fulfil it. When fashion designer Adam Lippes told friends he was going to start a T-shirt label, they were dumbfounded. It was, they told him, the very last thing the world needed. You can see their point. Next to jeans, the T-shirt is, after all, the most democratic fashion item. Every man and his dog wears them. And there's an overabundance of companies catering to every market niche, from expensive designer-label versions to cheap discount-store varieties. As a market, it's not so much saturated as sopping.

Or is it? Lippes spied a nice, wide gap — the quality staple.

There were plenty of T-shirts in crazy colours and patterns and every season there was something new. There are so many fashion T-shirts, but what really had been ignored was the very basic T-shirt that you could wear again and again.

Lippes wanted to produce a T-shirt made from quality cotton, and beautifully finished, that would be available — unchanged — season after season. But he is more than just an aficionado of the basics — high fashion is in his blood. Before starting his own business, he was the creative director at Oscar de la Renta, Hollywood celebrities' designer of choice for their red carpet turns. In fact, it was the high style of the de la Renta operation that spawned the new venture.

Lippes says he couldn't wear his favourite item of clothing — a V-neck white T-shirt — to such a dressy office.

> I found it very hard to find [a T-shirt] that I could wear to work that would look good and was really refined, but also basic in nature. I could sometimes find them at European fashion houses, but they were around $200 and it wasn't something you would want to buy lots of.

And so Adampluseve was born: a range of up-market, high-quality, perfect-fit T-shirts and underwear for men and women in a small range of plain colours that would be, as he puts it, 'not crazy expensive, but not cheap by any standard either. He wanted to make 'the perfect basic, the most perfect foundation'.

> I wanted to take underwear and T-shirts to a new level. Everything these days has been raised to another level. Today men and women are shelling out about $250 for a pair of jeans, but they are still spending $9 on underwear. When you buy underwear or T-shirts at that price they often fall apart after a few washes and are made from inferior fabrics. My idea was creating a new level.

Adampluseve has since been reborn and is now just 'Adam Lippes', but the underlying ethos hasn't changed. A basic T-shirt retails on the company's website for US$38.

For Lippes the success of his venture into the very crowded T-shirt and underwear market depended entirely on the fabric. 'The basis of everything was in the fabric,' he says. After researching cotton production and manufacturing in China, Colombia, Thailand, Italy, Portugal and Turkey, Lippes settled on a pima cotton from Peru, known for its extra-long 'staple' or fibre lengths. The long staple lengths allow for greater strength in a finer yarn, making the resulting fabric tougher and giving it a lustre.

It's one of the finest cottons in the world and has a lot of natural stretch, so it fits well. When the cotton comes out of the ground and is combed it actually shines and looks like silk. We then took it a step further and developed our own knit and also developed a special wash to give it that extra something.

Then came the ultimate market test: Lippes gave the T-shirts to his friends and colleagues to see what they thought – the same ones who were taken aback when he said he wanted to start a T-shirt business. One wear of his new super-soft cotton T-shirts and they were hooked. Lippes knew he was on to something.

His plain-coloured luxury T-shirts quickly became the favourite of the fashion and celebrity pack. According to Lippes his T-shirts are worn by Nicole Kidman, Jude Law, Jennifer Aniston, Brad Pitt, David Bowie and Ricky Martin, to name just a few. They have been

praised by industry publications such as *Women's Wear Daily* and fashion magazines such as *Harper's Bazaar* and *Elle*, as well as the mainstream press, including *The New York Times* and *Forbes* magazine. *The New York Times* couldn't even get past the packaging. In August 2004, just after the company's launch, the paper said:

> So luxuriant and glossy is the packaging for Adampluseve, so ostentatiously tasteful, that it is likely to define sales floor Eros today.

To be fair, the packaging does display imagery of men and women in their smalls that could make mere mortals feel inadequate. In 2006 Adampluseve's underwear was awarded best underwear in *Wallpaper\** magazine's design awards.

High praise and a flying start for a fledgling business, but Lippes's real big break came when his T-shirts caught the eye of Oprah Winfrey. The talk-show queen liked what she saw. Not that it got her any special treatment. 'She called and I left her on hold for about three minutes because I wasn't aware it was her,' recalls Lippes.

> She said she loved the T-shirts and wanted to know where she could buy more of them. Then, about a month later, one of her producers called and said 'Oprah would love to do something on you.'

After the resulting fifteen-minute segment aired in the US in May 2006, the Adampluseve website crashed as 50,000 people went shopping online simultaneously. In just two hours, Lippes did US$3.5 million worth of business. That was roughly 50 per cent of the company's projected annual internet sales at the time. What's more, the Oprah effect has been ongoing. Internet sales have since plateaued, but at ten times their pre-Oprah level.

Given his pedigree in high fashion at Oscar de la Renta, Lippes was well aware of the effect that getting your clothes on a celebrity's back can have. Nevertheless, when the Oprah thing happened Lippes kept his head on.

> We tried to prepare, but you just never know. We'd certainly heard about the Oprah effect, but as a small business, spending lots of money preparing for the unknown is risky. Being on *Oprah*, however, changed the scale of the business because suddenly people had heard of Adampluseve.

Born and raised in Buffalo, New York, Adam Lippes graduated from Cornell University with a degree in psychology and then spent a year at the American University in Paris, where he studied art history and architecture. He began his fashion career at Polo Ralph Lauren, then joined Oscar de la Renta in 1997, becoming the company's worldwide creative director at the age of just twenty-three. He started work on the concept for Adampluseve while still at Oscar de la Renta in 2003 and launched the brand the following year.

Oscar was wonderful enough to allow me to pursue my dream while being with him. After I had done my research into cotton and the T-shirts, I evolved that idea and did an entire business plan on paper, because ideas, no matter how great they are, tend to take money.

Oscar de la Renta recognised a good — and profitable — idea when he saw one and is now an investor in the business and on the company's board.

The Adampluseve concept was about a lot more than T-shirts, though. In February 2006, Lippes took part in New York Fashion Week, and presented a full fashion collection for men and women. The label had come a long way from its minimalist moorings: the collection featured fur vests, pintucked dresses with feather embroidery, and alpaca cardigans, but it was all part of the grand Lippes plan.

The fashion collection is really targeted toward the same customer who is buying the T-shirts. It all starts with the fabrics again — our customers are really style- and quality-conscious. All of our styles, they're fun, a bit preppy, but they are really basic in nature. It's meant to be a line that has simplicity at its core, but with very luxurious fabrics and great quality.

In a sense, Lippes went about creating a fashion label in reverse. Houses typically start with the showy, trendsetting end of the market and then, once established, offer customers the sort of basics — jeans and T-shirts — that make real money by reaping a premium for brand cachet. Instead, Adam Lippes has carried the original logic of luxury utility across into his more high-concept offerings.

'The idea was: why don't we start with the foundation of someone's wardrobe and build a fashion company around that,' says Lippes, who describes the label's high-fashion component as 'luxury basics'.

To that end, if a style of pants or type of knit is popular one season, he will bring it back the following season. 'I want to appeal to the customer who is on-trend but is not trendy,' he says.

The phenomenon of brands starting in one area and expanding into another has become popular. *Women's Wear Daily* has dubbed it 'crossing over'. Underwear labels such as Araks and Little Joe by Gail Elliott have recently moved into sportswear. Local designer Collette Dinnigan started that way too: she's a lingerie designer who crossed over into ready-to-wear. This has led some in the industry to remind labels that they need to continue to think smalls even as they act big. The senior vice-president and fashion director of Barneys New York, Julie Gilhart, cautions that such companies need to stay strong in their speciality if they want to be accepted.

Lippes agrees. If you're going to cross over you have to do it quickly, he says. But with caution.

> We started making sweaters in the second season and then we started making pants. Each season we added more until we had a full fashion collection. We've only been in business since 2004, so we are careful.

PHILIP TREACY

There is just a handful of fashion designers working today who, through their craftsmanship and mastery of technique, have become synonymous with the products they create. If you say to a fashion-literate person the word 'shoes', chances are they will immediately think of Manolo Blahnik. If you say 'handbag' it's quite likely that Louis Vuitton comes to mind; say 'silk scarves' and it simply has to be Hermès. Mention hats and there is no competition – Philip Treacy is *the* man you turn to. He is, in the words of *The New York Times*, 'the world's foremost milliner'.

His achievement is remarkable when you consider that hats have not been de rigueur for well-dressed women for decades. Until Treacy came along, hats were dowdy. The preserve of royalty and racegoers, they were about conformity with upper-class standards. This is what *Debrett's New Guide to Etiquette & Modern Manners* has to say on the subject:

Hats are pivotal to the woman's smart day wardrobe. They are de rigueur at weddings, Royal Ascot and other smart races. They are preferable but no longer essential at royal garden parties, christenings and other church services. Unlike their grandmothers, most women today are unused to wearing hats (particularly large ones) and are thus prone to spatial misapprehensions and clumsy collisions when meeting and greeting.

*Debrett's* goes into a great deal of detail on hat etiquette and how to deal with meeting and greeting while wearing one. As the standard-bearer of the British upper classes, it's hardly surprising that *Debrett's* would consider hats such an important item of clothing — and this is precisely why young people stopped wearing them in the 1960s. It was an act of rebellion against establishment mores.

In Australia, the biggest hat festival in the country is the Spring Racing Carnival in Melbourne, Victoria. In 1965 the English model Jean Shrimpton caused a sensation when she arrived for the Victoria Derby in a short white shift dress by Colin Rolfe with no stockings, no gloves and horror of horrors, no hat.

While Shrimpton was certainly something of a rebel at Derby day, she wasn't a lone figure. Hats had already fallen out of favour for everyday wear — and not just for egalitarian reasons. There was also a very practical reason for their decline: from the late 1950s, bouffant hairstyles and the popularity of wigs made it difficult for women to wear hats at all.

The genius of Philip Treacy is that he has not only made hats fashionable again, he has also managed to make the wearing of one a rebellious statement. He has taken a symbol of upper-class conservatism and turned it, quite literally, on its head.

Treacy, however, denies this.

Hats have been around since the beginning of time, you know, so I haven't exactly invented them. But when I started making hats in the late 1980s, hats were associated with Ascot and old ladies and Ascot hats were about jokes or something that was supposed to be funny. When I first started making hats people would phone up and say, 'Can you make me a hat that looks like a hamburger?' or something. And I'm like, 'Fuck off.' I'm interested in the kind of glamour hats can give, and what they can do for the wearer. It's that old movie star approach to hat wearing where they just looked better as a result of wearing one.

What I've brought to hats is that I've made them sexy. At the end of the 1980s hats certainly weren't sexy. No-one wanted to wear them and all the customers were old ladies.

Of course, the fact that hat-wearing was on the wane when Treacy came along only made their radical reinvention all the more possible.

His hats are part millinery, part architecture, part magic and part illusion. He has created hats that look like UFOs, hats in the shape of Romanov helmets, hats that resemble Campbell's soup cans *à la* Warhol and feather confections that defy description. Feathers are one of Treacy's favourite things to work with. 'I like to draw with feathers,' he says. 'I play with them until it feels right. Every arch and curve alters the balance of the lines.'

One of his most famous hats resembles an eighteenth-century French sailing ship. The inspiration, says Treacy, came from his discovery of a book about daily life in France in the 1750s called *Pleasure and Privilege* by historian Olivier Bernier. It was the custom of women in France at the time to wear model ships in their hair in celebration of victory at war; Treacy was intrigued.

> I always thought that it was just a costume designer's fantasy to show women with ships in their hair. What I liked about it was that it wasn't seen as funny. People applauded these women who expressed their political views by wearing something so extraordinary on their heads. So I decided to make this hat as a result of reading that. The hat is made entirely from traditional millinery materials such as feathers and feather bones.

It's all very well to make hats that look like ships or UFOs, but they need to find a wearer and they need to make that wearer look good rather than silly. Treacy found that person in Isabella Blow, while he was still a student at London's Royal College of Art. Blow (who died in 2007 at the age of forty-eight) was not exactly what you'd call a classic beauty, and she made up for it with her outlandish get-ups. She was the exception to the rule that the way fashion is presented on the catwalk – the sometimes ridiculous displays and bizarre styling – is not quite how it is intended to be worn. Blow was a great talent spotter and a true eccentric. She bought Alexander McQueen's entire graduate collection and saw nothing odd about wearing it exactly as McQueen presented it; she was a constant champion of his work.

Treacy was introduced to the then Isabella Delves Broughton in 1989. Treacy proffered a hat which Isabella later described in the pages of US *Vogue*:

> It was jaggedy green felt cut like the jaws of a crocodile – streamlined, chic, so exciting. I thought, 'This is major.'

She immediately commissioned him to design a hat for her impending nuptials to Detmar Blow in Gloucester Cathedral, for which she had chosen a medieval theme. Treacy suggested a wimple inspired by a costume worn by Lady Diana Cooper in the 1930s play *The Miracle*. Blow loved the concept, and Treacy was impressed:

I couldn't believe that I'd hit upon the one person who didn't expect tulle and veiling and pearls and such for her wedding hat.

Treacy says he had assumed the wedding commission would be a one-off collaboration.

But she rang me the next day when she was on her honeymoon and said, 'Tell me about the next hat you're going to make for me.'

The meeting of Treacy and Blow was a fateful one — one that changed Treacy's approach to hat design and, arguably, would eventually revolutionise millinery in general. In 2001, Treacy told *The New Yorker*:

If I hadn't met Isabella, my hats would have looked different. When Isabella's in your world, you just don't want to disappoint her.

The creative output of their relationship was celebrated in the exhibition 'When Philip Met Isabella', which has been shown in Melbourne, London and St Petersburg. It was Blow's attitude Treacy found inspiring:

What I love about Isabella is she wore hats as if it's not a big deal, it's as if she's not wearing one at all, which is the best way to wear a hat.

When Treacy and Blow met, she was style editor at *Tatler* and later went on to become the fashion director of London's *Sunday Times*. As a fledgling fashion school graduate, Treacy lodged at Blow's house. She introduced

her protégé to designers such as Karl Lagerfeld, Gianni Versace, Manolo Blahnik, Valentino and Rifat Ozbek, as well as fashion editors such as André Leon Talley of US *Vogue*. In 1991 Treacy was summoned to Paris by Lagerfeld to design hats for his Chanel haute couture shows, an assignment he held for ten years. The first hat he designed for Chanel was a twisted birdcage, which was worn by Linda Evangelista on the cover of British *Vogue*. Treacy went on to collaborate with Versace, Lang and Ozbek, as well as presenting fashion shows of his own.

The lofty heights of the fashion world were a long way from Treacy's upbringing. He was born in 1967 in Ahascragh, a tiny village in County Galway in the west of Ireland, with seven brothers and a sister. In 1985 he moved to Dublin to study fashion design at the National College of Art & Design. Smugly amused, Treacy tells me:

Nobody really had much time for the hat because it was a 'fashion' school, but there did come a point when I was more interested in making the hats rather than the outfits.

In 1988 he moved to London to study fashion at the Royal College of Art – with impeccable timing.

When I was interviewed I didn't know whether to play down the hats or play them up, but it turns out they were thinking of establishing a millinery course, so I became their guinea pig.

By 1993 Treacy had staged his own show during London Fashion Week and in 1994 he opened his own shop in London's Belgravia. In 2000 he was invited by the governing body of haute couture in France, the Chambre Syndicale de la Couture Parisienne, to present the first-ever haute couture show in Paris devoted entirely to headwear. His first Paris collection was of orchid-inspired hats.

Treacy also worked with the artist Vanessa Beecroft on an installation for the Venice Biennale in 2001, designed the interiors of the g hotel in Galway, Ireland in 2005 and, at London Fashion Week in 2006, launched a collection of men's and women's clothing in collaboration with the sporting goods company Umbro. Of his forays into other design areas Treacy says:

> I'd always concentrated on designing beautiful hats, but doing that gave me a sense of how good design can enhance any experience, from wearing a hat to staying in a hotel.

Despite this, millinery remains his foremost passion.

> What I like about hats is that you're making something from nothing. You know, you start with a two-dimensional material and you turn it into three dimensions.
>
> I studied fashion and I like fashion, but I've always liked to make things with my hands. In fashion you design something and then a

pattern cutter cuts it out and a machinist makes it. Whereas with a hat I can do it all myself.

When it comes to the question of Treacy's creative inspiration he is brutally frank.

Well, I can give you a lot of bullshit, but really it just comes. It comes from anywhere and anything. I can never really think about where it comes from. I like to sit down with a blank page and a pencil and draw and see what happens. And that's a very thrilling moment because you don't know what's going to turn up.

The conventional approach to studying fashion at college didn't always suit Treacy, especially when it came to the subject of inspiration.

At college you were taught to design through research and to go to the library. They would say things like, 'Today we are going to do a project inspired by the North American Indians.' Well I couldn't give a shit about the North American Indians. I like to design out of the blue and I'm attracted to things that I haven't seen before. If it reminds me of something else than I'm not really interested. The most exciting thing is to draw something and make it come to life.

Treacy likens the wearing of hats to cosmetic surgery and says the line of the brim of a hat can change the proportions of the face.

The magic in Treacy's often fantastical concoctions is that they are extraordinarily flattering.

> People have this idea that if they come into my store I'm going to make them walk out with a seventeenth-century sailing ship on their head, but they want me to make them look great and I want to make them look great and be happy. I don't want them to be disappointed, so I have to gauge their personality. It's a bit like being a psychiatrist sometimes. They want to look great and that's the bottom line.

The transformative effect the right hat can have on someone's face is something that Treacy learned at a very young age.

> I don't come from a fashion background by any means and my mother didn't have glamorous hats, but she wore hats, very simple hats. I remember as a child noticing that she would spend time looking in the mirror and adjusting her hat so that the angle of the brim was just right. She knew how to wear the hat and the angle of this very simple hat *was* the hat.

People just look better in hats, says Treacy:

> People behave differently in a hat. They stand differently and they feel good. I have incredible clients from all walks of life and they are all coming to me for the same reason, and that's because I make them

look good. With clothing, very few people look like a model should, and you're not going to look like one if you buy a particular dress. But everyone has a head and it's a really important part of the body to decorate because that's what you see first when you meet someone.

Given his frankness, not to mention his Irishness, Treacy is a somewhat improbable royalist, but he nevertheless credits the royal family for keeping hat-wearing alive. He has found an unlikely patron in the Duchess of Cornwall. Treacy has designed several hats for her, including two for her wedding to Prince Charles in 2005 – one of which was a gold-leafed feathered headdress, remarkably similar to a mirror on the wall of the Grand Salon in the g hotel. In the course of an interview with Treacy it's hard not to ask him the Camilla question. He laughs: 'That's all anybody wants to talk about these days.'

What's interesting about her [the Duchess of Cornwall] is that she doesn't wear old lady hats. She came into my shop about five years ago and I was late for our appointment and so she was alone in the shop with my dog, Mr Pig. Mr Pig was a Jack Russell terrier and he thought the shop was his and if he didn't like someone he would let you know. He was always growling at customers and when I walked downstairs to meet her he was sitting and staring at her adoringly and so I liked her from that moment on. They became great friends and she used to send him Christmas cards.

Decorating one's head is a tricky business. Treacy says customers need to put their trust in him, and insists he knows what he is doing.

> When people come to my shop — and I don't see every customer, but I used to — I can tell very quickly what is going to look good on them. They don't want to know really quickly though. They want to try on lots of different hats to arrive at the one that's best for them.

Treacy doesn't pull punches with his celebrity clients. When a wealthy and well-known woman approached him at an event he hosted at the Neiman Marcus department store in Chicago in 2005 and asked him if he could make her the same hat he made for Camilla Parker Bowles, he simply asked her 'Why?' He explains:

> I design different things for different people, so why make something you made for somebody else just because they can afford it? The hats I make for Camilla Parker Bowles are made with her in mind.

Another celebrity client is Oprah Winfrey who, says Treacy, orders about twenty hats a year. Now I discover that even Treacy's no-nonsense approach to dealing with customers has its limits:

> Oprah knows what she wants. She likes labour-intensive hats that look very special. She'll go, 'Philip, I like a brim and I don't want any feathers' and it's very hard to argue with Oprah.

Although the meeting of Philip Treacy and Isabella Blow was a match made in millinery heaven, even that had its difficulties. Blow revealed to the *New Yorker* in 2001 her bitter disappointment at receiving so little credit for Treacy's fame. 'In the Thames and Hudson book on hats, I'm not even mentioned,' she fumed.

> Boy George is there and not me. I resent it, really a lot. I asked Philip about it. I said, 'Why aren't I in the hat book? Why aren't I in your press releases?' No explanation. I might as well not even exist.

Despite the rift the pair remained friends. Treacy lovingly describes her now as the 'spanner in the works when people talk about the hats I created for her'. My interview with Treacy was conducted before Blow's suicide in 2007 (she had been diagnosed with ovarian cancer). I suggested to Treacy that Blow was a revolutionary when it came to fashion, but that after the revolution, it often seems that there is little left to fight for. He told me:

> What Isabella loved when I first started making hats for her was that nobody wanted those hats. And now it really annoys the hell out of her that people want the hat she's wearing, because in the beginning people wouldn't touch them with a ten-foot barge pole. But that's fashion – what's extraordinary becomes ordinary and that's the nature of how it works really.

KAREN WALKER

When I spoke to New Zealand–based fashion designer Karen Walker, she was just about to take on a new design assistant. Nothing new or extraordinary about that, you say. Except perhaps the way Walker went about recruiting her new assistant.

Walker's new assistant came courtesy of a scholarship initiative set up by Air New Zealand called 'Inspiring New Zealanders', which teams a relative newcomer who has plenty of talent with a fellow New Zealander already established as a leader in their field. As well as Walker, the filmmaker Martin Campbell (*Casino Royale*, *Vertical Limit*), winemaker John Belsham and several Olympic athletes are also taking part in the program. These mentors are not just providing some sage advice from time to time — these are not internships that Air New Zealand is funding, but full-time, permanent paid jobs.

The person Walker chooses will need to be more than just handy with a sewing machine. 'First of all they need to be able to design,' says Walker.

> Obviously we've got a big wish list. They need to be fast, efficient, a good communicator and able to work really well under pressure. They need to be able to do twenty-five things at once and not forget one of them. We're a little bit picky, but there are people out there who fit the description.

After we discuss Walker's philosophy of fashion it becomes clear what she is looking for in an assistant: a mini her. This is not meant to imply she's prone to narcissism; it's just that she expects her design assistant to be as passionate about fashion as she is. By her own admission, Karen Walker lives, eats, sleeps and breathes fashion. For Walker and her husband and business partner, Mikhail Gherman, it's more than just a job.

> I mean, we created a world for ourselves where what we do for a living is something that excites us and turns us on, but the cost of that is that it's also something that is with you all the time. As a creative person it's impossible to turn it off, and I wouldn't have it any other way.

Even when Walker is on holidays, she says, she emails her team and they reply in disbelief that she is working on her vacation.

But I'm enjoying myself. So what if I want to see my emails, or think about the next show, or start thinking about casting the models or whatever. I'm having fun. I wouldn't do it if I wasn't.

Potential applicants for the vacant design assistant position should have been warned: *you may get more than a full-time job*.

Still, what the successful applicant has now is the opportunity to work with one of the best design houses in New Zealand and possibly anywhere. Since launching her label in the early 1990s, Karen Walker has become one of the hottest names in international fashion for her dressed-down, quirky and feminine style. Walker has the uncanny knack of setting trends rather than following them, which might explain why she is a designer of choice for celebrities including Björk, Sienna Miller, Madonna, Jennifer Lopez and Cate Blanchett. She has more than 140 stockists around the world, including at least twenty in Japan alone; she's been featured in every major fashion magazine; and she shows her collections twice a year in New York.

In 2005 her London collection show was hailed by Worth Global Style Network (WGSN), one of the world's leading online research and trend analysis services for the fashion and retail industry, as one of the top five trend-setting collections for 2006. WGSN placed Walker's collection alongside high-profile brands such as Chloé, Lanvin, Miu Miu and Donna Karan and said:

Walker's collection . . . has creative commercial appeal without being pantomime, and illustrates that what London is about today is cool street-wear-inspired fashion labels that can more than hold their own with the likes of Undercover and Marc by Marc Jacobs.

After Walker's most recent New York show, Style.com praised her spring/summer 2008 collection for its eccentricity and sartorial whimsy.

Then there are her satellite brands: Karen Walker Jewellery, Karen Walker Eyewear and a range of house paints, created in collaboration with Resene, called Karen Walker Paints. She's also partnered with the New Zealand outdoors brand Swanndri, a sort of trans-Tasman R.M.Williams, to design a lifestyle line, and been involved in other design ventures including a make-up project with Boots in the UK and a T-shirt collaboration with the UK brand House of Holland.

She does it all far from the gravitational pull of the world's fashion capitals of Paris, Milan, New York and London. Walker is based in Auckland, New Zealand, in an outer suburb surrounded by bush — and it's another aspect of her life she wouldn't have any other way.

I'm a fashion designer who happens to live in New Zealand. The New Zealand thing is an easy descriptor and sometimes a point of difference that gets people's attention for about a quarter of a second, but it's not an indicator of style, any more than Marc Jacobs being an

American designer indicates his style. I really do think where I come from is irrelevant and the people who wear the clothes don't care about that either – all they care about is whether it's good.

Walker and her husband both work on the Karen Walker label, with Walker describing herself as the head designer and managing director and Gherman's role as more akin to that of a creative director:

His role is really overseeing everything at a sort of higher level. And I work with him on that, but then I'm also the driving force of the label. I get into the detail and make sure it's all happening and oversee everything and every stage.

As well as working on the Karen Walker label, Gherman has a full-time job in advertising as a creative director at Publicis New Zealand.

Both Walker and her husband agree that they could not have set up their business with their current model ten or fifteen years ago. The internet and improved telecommunications have enabled them to participate in a global industry from the far ends of the earth.

Obviously a designer like Christopher Bailey would not be able to do his job from Auckland, and I think if you're working for a big house then you have no choice but to locate yourself in a major city. But for us, at the stage we are at now, I do believe that we can do it from anywhere, as long as we are prepared to pack our little bags and get on a plane every now and then, or stay up late to take phone calls.

If New Zealand fashion has an identifiable style, it's probably best illustrated by a designer such as Elisabeth Findlay from Zambesi, whose clothes are often described as dark, emotional and brooding. Pieter Stewart, the managing director of New Zealand Fashion Week, likes to call the style 'defiantly different'. To put it bluntly, Karen Walker doesn't have that Kiwi look and it's doubtless what has enabled her to be such a major player in the international fashion industry. Walker herself says that participating in the global fashion industry while living in the forest of New Zealand is the very thing that has brought 'a certain casualness' to her work.

Where Zambesi is dark and intense, Walker is effortless and unpretentious. Her collections are best described as 'high casual' – we're not talking about red carpet evening gowns here. It's streetwear with a tailored edge. UK commentator Cat Callender once said that Walker's clothes have:

> . . . the kind of look that provides a means of appearing cool but not trying-too-hard, cute but not saccharine, alternative but not self consciously so. The fact that these clothes appear to be so totally not 'fashion' is what makes them so now.

Gherman describes Walker's designs as:

> . . . the kind of clothes that women can just wear. They can wear them on the red carpet if they want to or they can wear them every day. It's about the idea of the clothes being real.

However you choose to describe her appeal, Walker has a skill for designing clothes that women want. As for her muse? She looks no further than herself. 'One of the many criteria I go through when designing the collection is asking myself the question: Would I wear this?' she says.

> One of the reasons I got into this business is because I genuinely love fashion and I enjoy making it. I want to get my new clothes at the beginning of each season too, but I want to play in it and be part of the game as well. The whole thing gives me a kick. But beyond all that, what I really love about fashion is the opportunity to work in an industry that deals in ideas.

Karen Walker was born in Auckland in 1969 and left high school in 1988 at the age of eighteen, determined to embark on a fashion career. With her mother's old sewing machine and NZ$100 she set herself up in business while studying for a fashion diploma and made her first garment — a man's shirt in a Liberty print fabric. She sold it, made another, and within three years she had her first Auckland store.

By 1995 she had two stores. Then in 1998 she launched herself onto the international market with a show at Hong Kong Fashion Week. That same year she received the ultimate endorsement when Madonna chose Karen Walker pants to perform in at the MTV Awards. They were dubbed 'the killer pants' and almost took on a life of their own as Walker became known as the go-to girl for the ultimate in women's trousers.

Given that Walker's business and personal partner is an adman, it's no wonder she has been so savvy about extending her brand into other areas. Sunglasses and jewellery are hardly surprising areas for a fashion designer to get into, but house paint is another thing altogether.

> Fashion is not just about clothes. Fashion touches virtually everything in our lives in one way or another, so I felt like doing brand extensions to be able to tell our story in ways other than through women's clothing. It's all the same thing as far as I'm concerned, in that it's all about ideas, it's all about fashion and all about moving forward.

Walker's collaboration with the heritage brand Swanndri has extended her target audience: it now includes Kiwi farmers.

Swanndri started life in New Zealand more than 100 years ago with a showerproof bush shirt. In 1927, a hood and laced front were added to the original design, and it has been the mainstay of the company ever since. When Walker heard Swanndri had a new owner, it got her thinking. She approached them, and Swanndri by Karen Walker was born.

> It's not a fashion line, it's a lifestyle line. It's about longevity . . . it has an elegance to it but it's very much driven [by] quality. It's about the best cashmere scarves, the best picnic blankets, the best all-weather jackets, the best forty-eight-hour bag.

Walker says designing the range proved a welcome change of pace.

> As I was working on it I had to bear in mind that it would still be available in stores in five years' time, which is a completely different way of thinking to when you're designing high fashion where it has got to make a statement right now.

The venture has been an unmitigated success. In an April 2007 press release, Swanndri chief executive Julian Bowden said that the company couldn't keep up with demand for some of the T-shirts in the Swanndri by Karen Walker range.

Walker, however, is not about to go down the Pierre Cardin route and put her name on everything from underwear to, well, house paint.

> My feeling is that you can only do so much. I believe in getting in there and designing the product myself, so we have to limit it to one really big thing each year.

Then again, according to her husband at least, there's nothing that passes Walker's eye she doesn't have designs on:

> She's one of the only people I know who completes those suggestion forms you get when you check out of a hotel. And she will go on for three pages or more telling them exactly what they should change.

To create a truly international business, Walker needed to take her collections to the marketplace, rather than expecting buyers from department stores and exclusive boutiques to come to New Zealand and discover her. In 1999 Walker chose London as the place to show her wares.

> We chose London when we started because Paris and Milan just didn't feel right. We didn't really intend on showing in London either but our agent there twisted our arm and we ended up showing – and once you start showing you just can't stop.

After eight seasons showing in the UK capital, she moved to New York for her spring/summer 2007 collection. Reviewing the collection for Style.com, Tim Blanks said:

> The UK capital's loss was New York's gain as she showed a spring collection that was long on the skewed charm that's her signature . . . Walker's real focus, as always, was on the hybrid of female and

male. It's that fashion cliché about the woman who slips into her boyfriend's clothes in the morning, except in Walker's capable hands, it feels fresh and slightly subversive.

Fashion shows are expensive and nerve-racking, but, if you ask Karen Walker, absolutely essential.

It's an important way to show your idea in under fifteen minutes and everybody who needs to see it is there in the one room.

Mikhail Gherman, on the other hand, needed a bit more convincing.

I was kind of sceptical in the beginning to be honest. It's very stressful and for a designer it's a bit like a wedding day every time, but in actual fact it's just the easiest and quickest way to tell the story.

Telling a story and inventing a character is a device Walker uses to inspire herself each season, says Gherman:

What happens is we create a character, almost like a cinematic character, and then we dress them up for the different stages in their life. It's kind of semi-scripted, almost filmic in a way.

Walker adds:

Then we choose a name for the character, which is a little thing on the side that makes it easier for everybody working on the collection.

We like to be able to describe each collection in three or four words, so that the names of each collection capture the essence and the mood of it. For example, when we were doing our take on 1950s teen movies [in 2003], we called the collection 'Young, Willing and Eager', which was the name of a movie from the early 1950s. We felt the story behind that collection was sort of prom queen climbing out of the window after curfew, and we thought the name just captured the mood perfectly.

Other collections have been given titles such as 'Liberal and Miserable' (2004), 'Treegirl' (2005), 'Living with Cannibals and Other Adventures' (2005), 'Karen in TV Land' (2006) and 'Karen to the Rescue' (2007).

Naming the collections is primarily a way for us to convey a sense of adventure, but it's also saying something about the character that we're dressing for that particular adventure, that particular collection. For 'Living with Cannibals and Other Adventures' the inspiration was the idea of the 1930s aviator Amelia Earhart crash-landing on an island of cannibals and, perhaps, what she might wear for the occasion.

The titles of the collections are really just devices, says Walker. What comes first is the mood she wants for each season.

It's not like I say, 'Let's do a story about a girl lost in the woods.' That's not really the first stage, it's the second stage. What comes

first is the mood we want. Do we want it to be homely and cosy or do we want it to be sleek and tailored?

When we spoke, Walker was in the throes of finishing her autumn/winter 2006/2007 collection. At the beginning of work on this collection, Walker said, she found herself watching lots of 1920s cinema, including Marx Brothers films, and found that she loved the dark, grey, monochromatic colour palette of those films.

> The mood we came up with . . . was that the collection should be tailored, but it should be kind of crumpled, slept-in tailoring and it should be really dark and there shouldn't be a lot of colour, it should be quite grey and monochromatic. From there I have an idea in my head of what it should look like coming down the runway. And then we create the character from that. I had the idea that it would be sort of like cops and robbers. But my point is the mood comes first, then the character and her adventure and everything else.

Perhaps the character and storyline idea is a result of her adman husband's influence? Advertising executives like to be able to explain things in digestible grabs, and to be able to sum up the person they are trying to market to. It's the elevator pitch principle. You pretend you have stepped into an elevator with someone and you have only until you get to your floor to pitch them your idea. It's a handy device for summarising your sales spiel, and the comparison is not lost on Gherman.

> People ask us 'What's the collection, what is it?' And sometimes we have to communicate it in a sentence and be able to say, 'There it is.' Somebody called the other day from London and asked us what our idea for the next collection was. And really, you do have to tell them in one or two sentences because you just can't show it to them that quickly, being this far away.

Whatever the rationale for choosing a character and a storyline each season, the strategy appears to be paying off. In 2007, Walker's 'Dough and Dynamite' collection was well received by the media, described as 'well put together' and 'coherent'. Jess Cartner-Morley, fashion editor for *The Guardian*, said it was 'a show awash with great looks and nice running theme'. Tim Blanks summed it up for Runway Reporter:

> Walker's fashion signature gets clearer and more confident every season, especially in the sense of a woman casually incorporating elements of her man's wardrobe into her own.

Blanks thought the collection's name was particularly apt:

> Dough and Dynamite . . . should generate plenty of the former for Walker — as for the latter, I think the packed London audience would agree it went with a bang!

OZWALD BOATENG

To look at the British designer Ozwald Boateng you wouldn't think he was a stickler for tradition. London-born to Ghanaian parents, Boateng is known for wearing such things as a bright orange suit, or an electric blue, yellow, chartreuse or fuchsia suit. It's almost always a suit too, but even when he's chosen a more conventional sombre grey or black, there's really very little about the cut and silhouette that says 'traditional' to the casual observer. Except perhaps where his suits are made – Savile Row, London, the Ground Zero of British tailoring.

For over 200 years Savile Row in London's Mayfair district has been the bastion of British tailoring. It was named after Lady Dorothy Savile, the wife of the spendthrift third Earl of Burlington. When the earl was forced to sell the land behind Burlington House to pay his debts, a new pile of buildings was erected on the land. Not long after, the first tailors moved into the district and ever since, generations of gentlemen and the world's royal families have beaten a path there to be measured, with the utmost discretion, for the impeccable conservative suiting and military regalia for which the row is famous.

Winston Churchill, Lord Nelson, Beau Brummel and Napoleon III all patronised the tailors on Savile Row, as have the various incarnations of James Bond, as well as a who's who of the golden years of Hollywood — all of which has helped seal Savile Row's reputation as the ne plus ultra of gentlemen's fashion. To buy a Savile Row suit is to buy a garment that was made to your specific requirements. It's the closest thing in men's fashion to haute couture.

That proud history, those establishment credentials, make the sight of Boateng in his mod-cut, psychedelic-coloured suits all the more startling. And as you might expect of an industry so closely linked to the British establishment, Savile Row's tailors are not too keen on newcomers. Or change. Many of them still don't allow passers-by to enter and remain strictly 'by-appointment' businesses; many who do welcome the passing trade have refused to consent to modernism and open their doors on Saturdays. Some of the tailors on Savile Row have been in the same seventeenth-century row houses for over 200 years. Henry Poole & Co, which was the first tailor to open on the Row in 1806, is credited as the founder of the Savile Row tradition. In 2006 the company renewed its lease for another fifteen years, then did the unthinkable and refurbished its premises to bring them into the twenty-first century. Other tailors still in business can trace their lineage on the row back two centuries, including Huntsman & Sons and Anderson & Sheppard.

When Boateng came along and opened his first premises in the famed district in 1995, at 9 Vigo Street, which stares right down the barrel of Savile Row, he was seen by the established tailors as a mere pretender to the Savile Row tradition and not a welcome member of the club. In 2002, he closed the street to stage a fashion show in a 1500-person marquee erected down the strip, infuriating the old guard with his audacity. (To date, only Boateng and the Beatles have been given permission by the city to close the street. The Beatles' record company, Apple, was at number 3 Savile Row, where the band performed their final concert on the roof in 1969.) Today, however, Boateng is widely regarded as the designer who has not only taught an appreciation of fine tailoring to a new generation of men, but also rescued the tradition from virtual extinction, almost single-handedly.

One of Boateng's professional trademarks is the use of both traditional and non-conventional methods to create a vibrant yet formal look. In 1997, along with tailors Timothy Everest and Richard James, Boateng was christened the 'New Generation on Savile Row' by *Vanity Fair* magazine in its Cool Britannia issue. Boateng may not be the only new tailor to have opened on Savile Row in recent years, but of all the young British tailors who have spearheaded the renaissance of the craft he is the most charismatic and the most vocal. Boateng is acutely aware, and proud, of his own reputation, and isn't shy about discussing his achievements:

> You know I'm the first tailor to ever do a fashion show in Paris as part of men's fashion week and to make tailoring fashionable. And that sparked a revolution in the awareness of English tailoring. So I've been very much a pioneer in that way.

At several points in our conversation he referred to himself in the third person, as in 'That is very Boateng.' He is the row's self-appointed spin doctor, and doesn't hesitate to take credit for the resurrection of the Savile Row name:

> I've been an absolute revolutionary, you know. I've been really good for business here. I've been a huge promoter of the street. I put the street before myself and that's always been the case for me virtually from the day I opened shop here. I did, however, have to earn my respect as a tailor and as a creator of men's clothing on the street and that respect has grown over time [as people have recognised] the consistency of my work. I did experience some difficulties in the beginning, but I respected the row for what it was. In return I was respected for my work.

In 2006 Boateng was awarded an Order of the British Empire and, he says, he was knocked off his feet by the honour. 'Truly it was a very powerful experience,' he says. 'Pulling all those [other] achievements is fine, but to get that honour from the Queen just blows everything else away.' While Boateng is not the first Savile Row tailor to be honoured by the Queen – Savile Row tailors have been making garments for royalty since the trade started on the strip – the significance of his place in this lineage is not lost on him. 'It's not just the Queen giving you an honour, it's the history of the royal family giving you an honour.'

Boateng's apparent lack of modesty aside, there is no doubt he has been good for the strip. Sometimes, it can take someone new to shake things up and make people realise the traditions they have are worth holding on to.

> There is a real hierarchy here and certain people are accepted and others aren't. It takes an outsider to help the old guard value what they take for granted.

The practice of tailoring may have been invented in France, but Savile Row refined its techniques. Royal patronage ensured that the row would become as important to men's clothing as Paris was to women's. The traditions of men's bespoke tailoring – bespoke meaning literally 'by request' – echo those of haute couture. The client is measured, then a cloth prototype or 'toile' is created and adjusted at subsequent fittings. The fabric is hand cut and the canvas (the layer of cloth between the outer fabric and the silk lining) is sewn by hand. (A ready-to-wear suit would instead be 'fused', not hand sewn.) Savile Row has made some concessions to modernity over the years, such as using machines to stitch the longer outer seams, but otherwise all fabric is stitched by hand using the finest silk thread. A bespoke client can choose from thousands of different cloths and have their garment made to their specifications. The entire process can take up to eighty hours, with prices starting at around £3000.

In France, the term 'haute couture' has an exact definition, set out by the Chambre de commerce et d'industrie de Paris. Although the term is often abused by designers around the world, it has been protected by law since 1945 and its use is governed by very strict rules. A couture house must design and make to order clothes for private clients, with one or more fittings. They must have a workshop, or *atelier*, in Paris that employs at least fifteen people full-time. Each season they must present a collection to the Paris press, comprising at least thirty-five 'exits' (outfits) and including both day and evening wear. Only those companies 'mentioned on the list drawn up each year by a commission domiciled at the Ministry for Industry' are 'entitled to avail themselves' of the label haute couture.

The English have not been as diligent as the French in safeguarding

their exclusive right to such terms, but in 2004, recognising that the concepts 'Savile Row' and 'bespoke' were under threat of being devalued, Boateng and a group of other tailors from the strip formed the Savile Row Bespoke Association, with the aim of protecting and developing the art of bespoke tailoring as practised in the row and the surrounding streets. Before then pretty much anyone could add the word 'bespoke' or even 'Savile Row' to their label with very little retribution. Many tailors, some of whom had premises on the strip, were offering machine-made off-the-rack suits modified to fit a particular customer, and marketing it as a bespoke service. Since 2004 the association has been protecting the intellectual property of its member firms to ensure that the mark 'Savile Row Bespoke' is neither abused nor devalued.

Due to a historical quirk, all the row's leases were recently up for renewal simultaneously. The row's owner, the Pollen estate, in which the Church of England has a 65 per cent interest, allowed two of its biggest properties to be leased by high street fashion chains. The Japanese denim label Evisu opened a Savile Row store in 2005 and American clothing company Abercrombie & Fitch followed in 2006. Rents on the row subsequently skyrocketed and there were fears among the old guard that the street could soon turn into just another high-end strip mall. According to *The Times*, rents on Savile Row rose by 52 per cent between 1997 and 2004. Suddenly Ozwald

Boateng with his fashion parades and bright-coloured suits wasn't looking like such a bad bloke after all.

Boateng was born in 1968 in the North London suburb of Wood Green. His father was a teacher and instilled in his children a respect for personal presentation. According to Boateng his fashion calling came at the age of five when he got his first suit – it was double-breasted and made from purple mohair. (To keep up the tradition, for his visit to Buckingham Palace for his investiture, Boateng made his three year-old son Oscar a similar purple suit.) Boateng dropped out of a computer studies course at the age of eighteen and decided to follow his passion for clothing. By the age of twenty-three he was staging his own fashion shows and burst onto the world scene in 1994 with his first collection show in Paris. Just four years after that, however, his business hit the wall after more than £2 million worth of orders were cancelled as a result of the Asian financial crisis.

Today Boateng's business is going ever stronger. While his bespoke business accounts for only 10 per cent of his total business, there is a six-month waiting list to have an Ozwald Boateng bespoke suit made. The bulk of his business comes from his ready-to-wear line, which is manufactured in various factories and sold in several stores around the globe. His combined annual turnover is estimated to be worth more than £5 million. He has a women's line in the pipeline and has made a concerted push into the US market. In 2006 he was the subject of an eight-part reality television show on Robert Redford's US cable channel, the Sundance Channel, called *The House of Boateng*. The idea behind the TV show was to take his passion for bespoke to the MTV generation.

Boateng's fashion hero is, somewhat surprisingly, Giorgio Armani. Where Giorgio Armani made his name by taking the structure out of men's suiting, Boateng has made his by putting it back in. What Boateng admires about Armani is not just his reinvention of tailoring – though he sees himself as every bit the maverick that Armani was – but his creation of a clothing style that suited many different body shapes. 'Armani didn't reinvent Italian tailoring, he revolutionised tailoring around the world, full stop,' says Boateng with his signature hyperbole. In some respects Boateng sees himself as the inheritor of Armani's legacy and the next step in the evolution of menswear.

Armani invented this unstructured suit and he created a new way of wearing clothes for men, and what that enabled was the boom in ready-to-wear for men. The way he cut his suits meant that a lot of different people of various sizes could wear his clothes straight off the rack, which is what started the ready-to-wear revolution. What I've done is I've put the structure back in, but [that means] you can't buy my suits off the rack. And the reason why is I believe it's time for men to wear structured suiting again because it's more flattering to the male form.

Boateng stops short of drawing a comparison between his own philosophy of men's fashion and that of Hedi Slimane, who is also known for his slim silhouette, but whose ethos is that fashion and comfort don't necessarily go hand in hand.

I'm not as restricted as Hedi Slimane because I come from a tailoring background. You've got to make suits that fit men. The worst fashion mistake a man can make is wearing an ill-fitting suit. I'm famous for a slim-fit suit, but my version uses traditional tailoring skills that create a waistline that is very flattering and slimming. It doesn't necessarily mean that the suit fit is close – you just look slimmer in it. It's an illusion you create by knowing how to knock two inches off the waist and understanding where the break point on a lapel should be, and where you position the pockets, or the vent on a jacket. All of these measurements are key to creating a flattering form which gives the impression of a slimmer silhouette.

Like haute couture, there is a relatively small market for bespoke men's suiting. Although many Savile Row tailors will tell you that business is booming, the by-appointment nature of the craft and the fact that the suit is entirely handmade means there is a natural limit

to how far and how quickly the market can grow – or at least a limit to how long wealthy customers are prepared to wait for their suit. Boateng agrees with this judgement:

It's a completely insane business to be in, but I do it because I am passionate about it and it is really a labour of love for me. When you make a bespoke suit you are interpreting someone's needs. I've always been able to listen to what someone wants and to understand them and to bring my creativity to their demands. It's given me an interesting view on creativity. When I make something for an individual it's all about the relationship. And that's probably one of the big strengths of my brand, because if people know what they want and they like what I've created for them then they will tend to stick with me.

It's all about understanding the client's needs. Sometimes you get clients who are very clear about what they want and then you get some that are not so clear and then there are some that just need a little encouragement. It's a continuing balancing act, but I love the process.

I'm not as involved in all that as I used to be, but it is a great way to get to know your individual customers. I've always been blessed with a wide cross-section of clientele, from bankers to actors and pop stars, to scientists, you name it. Such a fusion of different characters and types of people means I've always had an interesting canvas, or range of colours, to work with.

Boateng insists that his bespoke business is a profitable one, with plenty of potential for growth.

> I've always believed that tailors are basically couture houses for men. In fact if you really looked at it you'd have to say they're *viable* couture houses. There's actually a future for couture houses for men, but there's less of a future for couture houses for women.

When you consider that the starting price of a couture gown for a woman is around €30,000 and a Savile Row bespoke suit might cost as much as £15,000, Boateng has a point.

Perhaps one of Boateng's greatest achievements is that he has made the men's suit sexy again. 'I have consciously done that too,' says Boateng. 'I have always wanted to create sexy clothes for men.' No doubt it was his knack for making something conventional seem sexy that drew him to the attention of the luxury group Moët Hennessy–Louis Vuitton in 2003, when he was asked to design the Givenchy menswear range. The collections he did there were well received by the media, but failed to sell. It was classic men's suiting, but *not* bespoke, which is a tough market to compete in because there are so many designers doing it. In January 2007, Givenchy announced it had 'scaled back' Boateng's role in the brand. Whatever that means, it hasn't stopped Boateng on his personal quest to get men out of track pants and into bespoke suits.

'People often ask me why I do it,' says Boateng in reference to the notoriously difficult business of menswear.

I don't know why the hell I do it to be honest. You know, I've heard about these climbers who try to climb Mount Everest and I often wonder why. It takes such belief and passion to be crazy enough to climb Everest, and that's what it is like for me. I've been given many options to do different things in my career and I chose every day to climb Mount Everest. What was I thinking?

AKIRA ISOGAWA

Akira Isogawa is a quiet, Zen-like person; he only ever wears simple clothes, mainly in solid colours, and he speaks of the 'transcendental power' of fashion. Then, of course, there's his background. Isogawa grew up Kyoto, the ancient capital of Japan, surrounded by Buddhist temples and imperial gardens designed to encourage Zen thoughts. So it is something of a surprise to discover that his work environment is anything but Zen-like.

On the day of our interview, the lift in his building was on the blink, so visitors were forced to climb the stairs and navigate the rabbit warren of a building, tenanted by a number of fashion businesses, in which he has his studio. Welcome to the garment district of Sydney's Surry Hills. The white door with 'Akira' written on it in Isogawa's handwriting is Zen enough, but that's where the peace and serenity begin and end.

The door opens onto a large workroom. After I find someone to greet me, I am ushered to a small table and chairs set up among the racks of clothes. As I sit and wait for Isogawa, a heavy thud on the floor above can be heard through the whirring of sewing machines. It's loud enough to send me bolt upright, but no-one else seems to hear it.

Then the heavens open up and water starts cascading through the cracks in the floorboards above me. I can't seem to get anyone's attention so I start to move the clothes on the rack directly underneath the waterfall to one side so that they won't get damaged.

When Isogawa's assistant comes to fetch me for the interview I tell her what just happened. 'Oh that's just someone upstairs knocking over a vase of flowers, I suspect,' she says, matter of fact. Could it be that Isogawa and his team are so focused on producing beautiful clothes that water pouring through the ceiling is too trivial to worry about? After all, Isogawa is a designer who speaks of such things as the 'soul of a dress'. When our interview finally gets under way, he tells me:

A garment can transcend being just a garment, giving it a soul. I translate fabrics into soft, romantic silhouettes and I use natural fibres only, which are nicer and kinder to the skin . . . Timeless beauty and femininity in my design is profound – my clothes are a way for the wearer to express their inner soul.

FASHION SPEAK

He is softly spoken, charming and gracious, and it's only towards the end of the interview that he warms up and allows his keen sense of humour to show through. Unassuming courtesy is rare in such a cut-throat business. Isogawa, however, is one of Australia's most successful designers and has achieved international recognition for his collections, which are stocked in stores in London, New York, Paris, Tokyo and many other cities. He was the subject of a major exhibition at the National Gallery of Victoria in 2004/05 called 'Akira Isogawa: Printemps–Été', which charted the creative journey behind the production of his spring/summer 2005 collection. The exhibition later travelled to Singapore, Manila and Bangkok. In 2005 he also received an accolade usually reserved for sportspeople in Australia: he was immortalised in a stamp as part of Australia Post's 'Legends' series.

Such triumphs are a long way from his humble beginnings as a fashion designer. When he made his debut as part of a group show at Australian Fashion Week in 1996, he couldn't afford shoes for his models, so he sent them down the runway in red socks. Today he shows his collections in Paris twice a year, but the Isogawa show remains one of the highlights of the Australian Fashion Week schedule. Tickets are sought after, due to his unique presentations and collaborations. In 2005, for example, Isogawa asked dancers from the Sydney Dance Company to dance in and model his clothes on the runway.

Isogawa is something of a workaholic. He is, he says, almost always working, even if it's just thinking about his collection.

I have so many ideas all that time that it is frightening. There are lots of ideas and design for me is just choosing which idea is relevant to what I am doing.

Being so driven has its drawbacks. Rest is important: Isogawa says he needs a healthy body in order to have a healthy mind.

If inspiration doesn't come, then it doesn't come. I deal with it by just not doing very much. When you don't feel inspired there's really not much you can do about it. It's better for me to just stay still and eventually when the body and mind is rested it will come. My normal state of mind is feeling inspired, so if I'm not feeling inspired then I know there's something wrong with my system and I've got to do something about it.

When we spoke, he had just returned from an overseas trip.

At the end of May after Paris I was so exhausted that I just thought, I cannot find inspiration like this, so I decided to leave the city and I went to India.

The first thing I did when I got on the plane was to go straight to sleep. Sometimes I just need to leave Sydney, even if it's only for

a few days, because I feel that I need to refresh my brain and get stimulated by something. Travelling is a great way to do that.

Isogawa uses his overseas trips for research as well as inspiration. Apart from his twice-annual pilgrimage to Paris, most of Isogawa's travel is to Asian destinations where he can recharge his battery and also investigate traditional handicrafts and textiles.

I visit a lot of different cities in India, but I like Calcutta, where there is workmanship that is handcrafted. For example, if the fabric is dyed by hand, using a dye that was also made by hand, rather than dyed on a mass scale, then that for me is a textile that is more personalised and more organic, which is what I like.

Because I've been to places like Calcutta this season for inspiration, you could definitely say that my work is more Indian as a result, but it is really the type of workmanship that I feel connected to. I like to be able to modify things and apply my own aesthetic to their expertise.

In spring/summer 2006, the Indian influence came through, he says, in the hand printing, hand sewing, hand pleating and hand embroidery he used, but the collection overall was 'about exploring ideas and different techniques on textiles to create a unique texture and combining different textures and colours together.'

For Isogawa the fabric comes first. The shapes and silhouettes of the garments he designs are dictated by the textiles he discovers. 'I have tried many cities in Vietnam,' says Isogawa of his constant quest for new textiles.

> I give them [Vietnamese handicraft producers] a small portion of the collection to try and see how the garments they make come out. And from there the collection starts to get built.

The Vietnamese producers make completed garments for him, but not the entire collection each season – just a portion of it.

Isogawa clarifies:

> I only do small portions of the collection with these companies because I prefer to work with machinists and cutters face to face rather than via email. I try to personalise my style as much as I can so it's important to have an intimate environment.

Unique, personalised textiles have been integral to Isogawa's work from the beginning of his career. Isogawa was born in Kyoto in 1964 into a family in which traditional values reigned. As a child he watched his mother and grandmother hand sew their kimonos. Many of Isogawa's early works incorporated vintage fabrics, often from kimonos, reinterpreted as contemporary garments. Today vintage kimonos are increasingly harder to come by, not to mention

expensive. Hence Isogawa's travels throughout Asia to find the right craftspeople to create his unique fabrics.

He moved to Australia in 1986 and backpacked around the Northern Territory and Tasmania before settling in Sydney and working as a tour guide. Sydney's op-shops fascinated Isogawa: he saw in them a stark contrast to Japan and its consumerist hunger for the new. When asked why he decided to leave Japan, Isogawa says:

> . . . because I am a very curious person and Kyoto is such a traditional city. It is still common to see women wearing the kimono in Kyoto. My brother went into a career in finance and I felt I had to suppress my desire to study art — my family was far too conservative.

He enrolled in the fashion design course at the East Sydney College of the Sydney Institute of Technology. After graduating he started making clothes and selling them to various boutiques around the city. In 1993 he opened the first store bearing his name, in Queen Street, Woollahra, in Sydney. His show at the inaugural Australian Fashion Week in 1996, the one with the red socks for shoes, drew positive responses from critics and buyers alike. Since then he has launched a menswear line and a diffusion line called Akira Red which includes a range of customised Bonds singlets that retail for about $80. Isogawa has also joined forces with Designer Rugs to create a series of luxury carpets featuring some of the kimono motifs he has used in the past.

In Paris Isogawa shows his collections to key buyers in a low-key showroom format rather than in a runway show, which can cost hundreds of thousands of dollars. However, he is not ruling out the prospect of a Paris runway show. 'It will happen sooner rather than later, but sales have to accommodate the expense of the show.' Isogawa says exports of his label now account for 70 per cent of his business.

An expanding business and new product lines can take their toll, especially when the designer likes to design everything that comes out of his studio personally. Although Isogawa has people around him to help him with the non-design side of things, he still maintains it's very difficult running a business.

> It's hard to find the time to sit down and then start working on design, but if I don't design then the company won't exist. The people who work for me understand that. So when I suddenly think, oh my god, I haven't done anything about the new collection, and I tell them that I need to be left alone for a while, they do. Otherwise it would all stop. If there's no collection there's no company.

Although he no longer incorporates sections of vintage kimonos in his work, he still shows a Japanese sensibility in his use of layering and incorporation of contrasting fabrics. He eschews the conventional techniques of Western tailoring to produce loosely structured garments.

Some people have criticised my work for lacking construction. But the clothes reflect what I feel about the women who wear them and I think that's what makes my designs Australian.

In some ways Australia has been as important an influence on Isogawa's aesthetic as Japan has. He says he can remember when he was young and his mother stopped wearing the kimono and adopted Western dress. Because of that he always thought of the kimono as old-fashioned. It was only when he arrived in Australia that he found new inspiration in their design.

The kimono looked so different under the Australian sun that it made me identify it with modernity rather than tradition, and that's what inspired me to use kimono in my womenswear collections.

Isogawa is a keen people watcher and says that his observations of women in particular help form his collections.

I observe women every day and their behaviour and how they look on different occasions. And I think about their personalities and the style of clothes that [an individual with a particular sort of] personality usually wears. For me it is actually a process of identifying what I don't like, which gives me a good idea of what I do like. I think about personalities that I like to spend a lot of time with. For example, I don't like very aggressive women with high heels and damaged, blow-dried hair — they make me feel scared. So I think aggressive-looking clothes are not tasteful.

Few fashion critics doubt Isogawa's ability and talent as an artist, but it's a tag he's not all that fond of. With his two labels — Akira and Akira Red — his designs have moved to two extremes, echoing a broader trend in the global fashion business. His high-end label, Akira, is more experimental and more expensive; Akira Red is no less creative but certainly more commercial. 'We've got to generate income,' says Isogawa of his decision to start a diffusion line.

It's very nice when people say my clothes are wearable art, but my answer is 'No, they're clothes.' I'm a fashion designer, I'm not an artist. What I do is sell clothes.

# ELISABETH & NEVILLE FINDLAY

## ZAMBESI

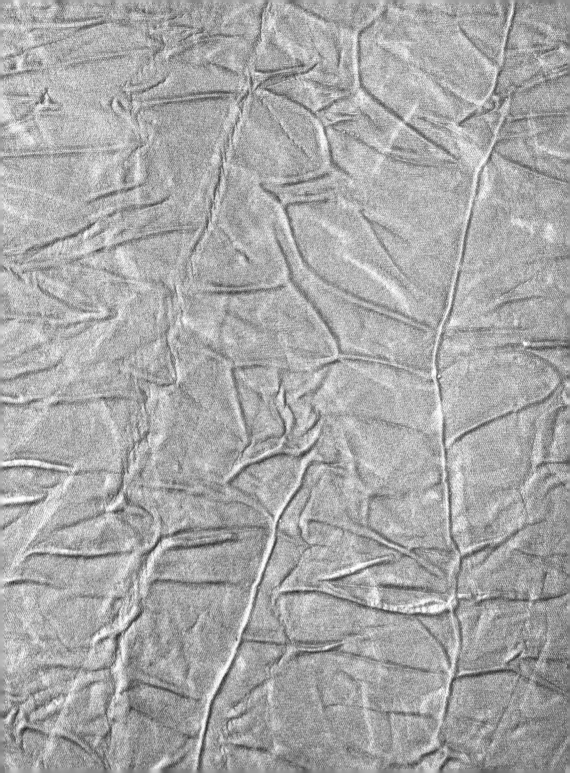

To truly get an idea of what the nearly 30-year-old New Zealand fashion label Zambesi is all about you really need to see it in context — that is, in New Zealand. Although the label, designed by the husband and wife team of Elisabeth and Neville Findlay, has shown its collections in Sydney, Melbourne and London and is stocked in stores in Australia, the United States, the UK, Russia and throughout Asia, on its home turf is where it really shines.

I attended the Zambesi show in Auckland during New Zealand Fashion Week (NZFW) in 2003 — definitely one of the more innovative events of the week. In retrospect, the invitation to the show was a harbinger of what was to come. When an invitation to attend a fashion show advises you to dress warmly, you know you're in for something out of the ordinary.

**ELISABETH & NEVILLE FINDLAY**

It was held at night in the abandoned Oriental Markets building down by the harbour's edge. Spectacular graffiti adorned the walls and many of the windows were smashed. Although it was dark and cold inside, the Zambesi show was the hottest ticket on the NZFW schedule. Elisabeth and Neville Findlay were about to show why they are the undisputed queen and king of New Zealand fashion.

A long white 'catwalk' was painted down the middle of a floor the size of a football field and flanked by rows of benches. And just as it was a long walk for the models down the runway that night, it had been a long journey for the Findlays to reach this point. They are the quiet achievers of New Zealand fashion – preferring just to get on with the job, rather than counting column inches or courting celebrities to wear their clothes. They have earned their pre-eminence through hard work and an original, unswerving vision.

In the front row that night was Colin McDowell, fashion historian and senior fashion writer for London's *Sunday Times*. McDowell had come all the way to New Zealand to see if the lacklustre mood at Australian Fashion Week (AFW) months earlier was a result of a drop in the number of NZ designers showing there. He was wondering if the buzz had crossed the Tasman. It had, he decided. His pick of the week was Zambesi.

Colette Garnsey, David Jones's general manager for apparel, felt the same. The clincher for Garnsey in deciding to back Zambesi in 2003 was seeing the label in its home market, she says.

Neville Findlay, who looks after the business side of things while Elisabeth designs the clothes, says that New Zealand show sealed the deal for other overseas buyers too.

> All the success we've had in the UK was when the label has been seen in New Zealand in context. When international buyers have come down and been in our store and our showroom it's been a big hit. They get a bit of a take on what New Zealand's about and what the label's about.

The label experienced such strong export growth as a result of the 2003 parade that the company had to appoint agents in Europe and the United States to manage demand from retailers in those markets wanting to stock the label. Exports now account for a significant percentage of the total business, and in 2005, at the same time that a retrospective exhibition of the label was staged at the Auckland Museum, its annual growth rate was about 25 per cent.

Pieter Stewart, managing director of NZFW, says she's not meant to have a favourite when it comes to NZ designers — but if she had to pick one, Zambesi would be it.

Jane Roarty, former fashion editor for *Harper's Bazaar* and now executive fashion editor for *Marie Claire,* says:

> I think of Zambesi as like the Belgians of the Asia-Pacific. They have a very strong philosophy. It's not just about the clothing. It's about where they come from and their culture.

Elisabeth Findlay agrees that her environment has shaped her approach to design:

> It's because New Zealand is isolated that we don't have the pressure of influences that would be all around you in Europe, for instance.

New Zealand's disconnection from the larger world of fashion has prompted many people to compare what's happening with design there to what happened in Belgium in the late 1980s and early 1990s. The Antwerp Six, as they came to be known – Dirk Bikkembergs, Martin Margiela, Ann Demeulemeester, Dirk Van Saene, Dries Van Noten and Walter Van Beirendonck – sent fashion commentators into a frenzy with their unique design aesthetic and stole the limelight from the established fashion houses of Paris and Milan.

The Findlays' geographic isolation has not led them to be inward looking. On the contrary, like fellow New Zealander Karen Walker, they prefer to see themselves as international. Neville explains:

Yes, there is a kind of New Zealand outlook to design. But I also think in New Zealand we try very, very hard to be international, because of our isolation.

Elisabeth puts it another way:

I think New Zealanders strive for excellence. They want to prove they are international and that they can do what they do anywhere. The first time I went to Japan, it was only about three years after I started Zambesi, and when I saw the quality and the standard of workmanship in their designs it really impressed me and it made me think, I have to try and be as good as that, to stand alongside that.

Zambesi first showed at Australian Fashion Week in 1997. At the time Elisabeth felt out of her comfort zone, and also thought the event was hype-driven, but she says, 'We felt we were international and part of something really big. It was a great feeling.'

Her designs for Zambesi are an idiosyncratic mix of fabrics, layering techniques and a finely tuned instinct for tailoring. She eschews the trends du jour and designs garments that are intended to be worn for several years. 'Zambesi really has its own point of view, a view that . . . Elisabeth Findlay has always been true to,' says Fiona Lane, former senior fashion editor for *Vogue Australia* and now fashion director for *Madison* magazine:

She has a great sensitivity for colour, print and texture — the way she mixes and layers her clothes creates a completely unique aesthetic that is intricate but with a masculine edge. Also, the clothes accommodate all ages, as the core of the collection is always based on beautifully conceptual, yet wearable, pieces.

Elisabeth Findlay says she never feels the pressure to come up with something drastically different each season. With an archive of designs spanning more than twenty-five years, she's not afraid of revisiting some of her greatest hits from time to time.

Quite often Tulia [a long-time member of the Zambesi team] will say to me, 'I still love that old thing I got when I first started here,' and so we'll drag it out and look at it again, or reinvent it in some way.

I really feel that one of the strengths of the brand and what has helped to give it its longevity is the fact that there is not that radical shift each season. We're not asking our clientele to take a quantum leap every time they come into the store. They get a certain feeling when they wear our clothes and we don't want to play with that too much.

Neville agrees:

It's an evolutionary process. I mean the last five collections could almost be considered one long collection which gets added to and subtracted from each season.

Despite the esteem Zambesi is held in by those in the industry, Elisabeth is not precious about her label and not prescriptive about how people should wear it. Where some designers would like to see their customers in one label head-to-toe, Elisabeth says she's not fussed if people wear Zambesi with other labels — she even encourages it. The Zambesi stores in New Zealand, in fact, are multi-brand stores stocking other designers such as Martin Margiela and Dirk Bikkembergs. The whole point of her clothes is that they don't scream 'Zambesi'. She tells me that there's 'a real question about the label'.

> 'What is that? Is it Zambesi?' I like the idea that it isn't blatantly one look. I have a passion for clothing and that embraces more than just Zambesi.

For better or worse, her clothes fit the frequently used descriptions of New Zealand fashion: quirky, cerebral and dark. But these epithets don't bother Elisabeth.

> I think there is a dark side and I think that also comes out in music, film, writing and many areas of art. It's a good thing — it's being deep and emotional.

Neville questions whether New Zealand fashion is actually dark, but insists that it does have an intellectual side.

> Probably because of New Zealand's isolation and because we had to be self-sufficient for many years [due to] import restrictions, we have developed an individuality.

He thinks New Zealanders and Belgians have developed this individuality for similar reasons, though the distinctive national styles that have emerged as a result are very different.

Elisabeth Findlay's interest in clothing was inherited from her mother, who worked as a machinist in the rag trade. Her parents, one Greek and one Ukrainian, moved to New Zealand as Red Cross refugees after World War II, eventually settling in Dunedin, where they raised six children. Elisabeth left school at fifteen and by twenty-one had moved to Auckland, where she got a job with a clothing manufacturer and learned the business from the bottom up. She met Neville, an industrial designer, on a blind date in 1969. The pair married a year later and opened their first Zambesi shop in 1979.

Back then they were strictly retailers, stocking a wide range of labels. But it didn't take long for Elisabeth, a self-confessed fashion victim, to start making her own designs to sell in her shop. The ratio of Zambesi to other designers quickly shifted to the point where Zambesi became a fully fledged label in its own right, but the Findlays maintained their relationship with the designers they stocked, including Martin Margiela, whose clothes they have carried for over ten years, largely because they like what he does. 'It's been a love of ours and it's really a respect thing,' says Neville.

Elisabeth's younger sister, Margarita, still lives in Dunedin, where her label NOM*D is based. The sisters travel overseas together to buy fabrics for their respective labels and have carved up New Zealand between them for their burgeoning retail empire. Margarita has the South Island, with NOM*D shops in Christchurch and Dunedin that also stock the Zambesi label. The Findlays have the North Island, with three Zambesi shops in Auckland and one in Wellington, all of which stock the NOM*D label. There are also Zambesi stores in Sydney and Melbourne which mainly stock the house label.

Like many fashion designers, Elisabeth sees choosing the fabrics as the starting point for any collection.

> For me it's the fabric that inspires me – I find the fabric first and then I create with it. It very much begins with the fabric and the colour palette and then I decide where we're going with it and what kinds of garments we're going to make with it.

As well as re-working old designs, she says, the Zambesi team love to re-use and re-interpret fabrics from previous seasons.

I also love old fabrics and old clothes. So we're quite often reinventing something that we've used before, maybe re-colouring it, enlarging the print or minimising the print. It's about manipulating things that we've used before or that have come from the past.

Unlike many of the other fashion designers featured in this book, Elisabeth Findlay works closely with a real, live muse. Tulia Wilson started her career with Zambesi on the shop floor when she was nineteen years old and gradually progressed to a visual-merchandising role. Wilson recalls:

I used to go into the workroom every week . . . and it was much more exciting [than the shop], all this creativity going on, and I always found it very interesting.

Elisabeth tells me how Tulia grew more involved with the business:

Tulia came up and started working with Neville for half the week – they worked together on marketing and all kinds of things – and then that grew into a full-time position.

No-one seems able to articulate what Tulia's exact title is these days, but Elisabeth says they work together closely.

Sometimes I just grab Tulia and say, 'Go pop this on' and then I'll actually work with it on the body. Sometimes it's the fabrics that

inspire me, but sometimes it's the women around me, because we're all very passionate about clothes and we're all thinking all the time about how to change something and so we're always bouncing around ideas. I really rely on Tulia quite a lot – she is just amazing. She has always been incredibly willing to be pushed and pulled as I take to what she is wearing with a pair of scissors.

It might seem that Wilson would be the logical successor to Elisabeth Findlay to keep the Zambesi label going, should Findlay decide to retire, but the Findlays' daughter Marissa *also* works in the business – on the press side of things. Then there's the Findlays' squad of long-serving staff members, many of whom have been with the company for over a decade and are the backbone of their business. Their pattern maker, for example, has been with them for fifteen years, and the head sample machinist for ten. Both have grown accustomed to the way Elisabeth thinks. 'The whole process is collaborative in the end,' says Elisabeth.

After almost twenty-five years of successfully designing womenswear, in 2003 Zambesi launched its first full men's collection, under the direction of designer Dayne Johnston. Neville explains why they made this move:

Menswear is not an easy market but we went into it with our eyes open, because it has huge potential internationally. And it does give us a lot of cachet when we're exporting to have a complete collection, to have an offering in both men's and women's wear.

Johnston works closely with Elisabeth on the menswear so that the two collections sit next to each other comfortably. He observes:

> There was quite a demand for a men's equivalent from our female customers, who were encouraging their partners to dress with the same aesthetic that the women's line represents. Quite often the fabrics cross over both ranges. Liz likes to use beautiful masculine suiting fabrics in the women's range, so they work quite well in the men's range too.

The Findlays are by no means resting on their laurels. In 2005 they unveiled the uniforms they designed for Air New Zealand after winning a competitive tender which pitted them against other New Zealand designers. Neville Findlay described the process as 'a most satisfying experience'.

> You would be amazed at the different parameters that get chucked at you when you do something like this. From climate considerations to fire safety to functionality and the myriad other things you have to take into account, and then you have to come up with something stylish.

Instead of the label's signature dark palette, Elisabeth opted for lighter shades of teal, stone and slate to reflect the country's landscape.

The Findlays, according to NZFW's Pieter Stewart, are also incredibly generous with their time and expertise and worked with her on the organising committee for the inaugural national fashion week. In 2007 Zambesi sponsored the Young Designer of the Year awards in New Zealand, with the winner of the student award receiving an internship with the company, under Elisabeth's guidance.

Back in 2003, a few days after the Findlays' standout show at the Oriental Markets building, I saw evidence of this warmth and generosity firsthand. Across town on the Wednesday night it was Margarita Robertson's turn in the spotlight with her label NOM*D. The clothes were a long way from the Zambesi style: sweatshirts, hooded tops, Soviet-era graphics screen-printed onto T-shirts and lots of red. The show was well received, but when it finished there were just as many people trying to get a moment with Elisabeth and Neville as there were with Margarita. True to form, the Findlays scurried off backstage to leave NOM*D in the limelight.

When pressed about their achievements and staying power in an industry known for its hyperbole, Elisabeth is remarkably modest.

We never had a big plan and we never set out to become an established label. We didn't envision it getting to this stage. It's really just grown

ELISABETH & NEVILLE FINDLAY

on its own with us in the steering position, I suppose. Our attitude is that we take opportunities as they come along. If it works, that's great. If it doesn't, it's no big deal. It's always a process of evolution.

It's almost as though they've held themselves back to ensure their longevity in the business.

The next step is taking the Zambesi label to the rest of the world. The Australasian market has long been the primary focus, but Neville says their success with NZFW has inspired them to try and make it big in the potentially lucrative Northern hemisphere market.

> By virtue of the maturity of the company we've got some momentum and we're a bit of an institution in New Zealand. In the rest of the world we're very little known.

Now they have stockists in the UK, the Findlays are looking at breaking into the US market. It's an uncharacteristically hard-headed move. For the last twenty-five years they've been content to go with the flow. Now they have to think seriously about things such as marketing and PR — areas of the business they have long shied away from. In late 2005 Zambesi was the principal recipient of the $55,000 Air New Zealand Fashion Week export award. Neville tells me that the in-kind award is designed to help offset the expense of foreign travel, offering accommodation at Hilton Hotels and shipping by DHL.

To win this award we had to provide a specific business plan for a specific area of export activity, and we have based ours around the United States, in particular California and New York, where we are receiving quite a bit of interest at the moment.

Elisabeth adds that they are considering following in the footsteps of other antipodean designers such as Karen Walker, Josh Goot, Kit Willow and Toni Maticevski by showing their collections overseas regularly.

For Zambesi we think it could possibly be New York where we would choose to show, but then Paris would definitely be an option too.

Exporting is not without its difficulties and the road to the international marketplace for antipodean fashion designers is paved with potential disasters. With the cost of freight and import duties, Zambesi is priced in the same echelon as Martin Margiela and Helmut Lang in stores in the UK and the US. But Elisabeth is unperturbed.

The market is huge over there and we're happy that there are opportunities for someone who wants to embrace the label and who identifies with it. It's there for the passionate, really.

# NICOLE & MICHAEL COLOVOS

## HELMUT LANG

In 1997, Helmut Lang went on record in *The St. James Fashion Encyclopedia*, saying that his aesthetic was 'all about today'.

> It has to do with my personality, with my life and with the idea that quality doesn't go out of style every six months.

Fashion is all about change, but when Lang spoke those words he probably never expected quite the level of change that was about to befall him. Only a couple of years later, he sold 51 per cent of his business to the Prada Group. By October 2004 he had sold the remaining stake to Prada and by the following March he had resigned altogether from the company he had founded. To add insult to injury, by the end of 2005 all that remained of the Helmut Lang business was a few trademarks – Prada had ceased production, saying that the label had never made a profit under its stewardship.

NICOLE & MICHAEL COLOVOS

Then in March 2006 Prada sold the Helmut Lang brand to the Tokyo-based Link Theory Holdings for an estimated €20 million. The Helmut Lang sale came just weeks after Prada sold off the Jil Sander label to the private equity company Change Capital Partners after a similarly torturous marriage. Link Theory Holdings clearly thought there was still life in the brand, and hired husband-and-wife design team Michael and Nicole Colovos to run it.

Given that Lang once said the label was a reflection of *his* life and *his* personality, with a new owner and new designers calling the shots, it begs the question: whose life and whose personality does it now reflect? The board of Link Theory Holdings? Nicole and Michael Colovos? Some sort of channelling of Helmut Lang?

Before we get to the answer, it's worth considering the circumstances that led to Michael and Nicole Colovos being installed as the new designers of the Helmut Lang label.

If Marc Jacobs is *the* success story when it comes to managing the friction between art and commerce in today's fashion industry, the story of the demise and subsequent rebirth of the Helmut Lang best personifies the pitfalls of working within the globalised fashion system.

The promise of being part of one of the major fashion and luxury conglomerates is that the investment they can make in the smaller brand will result in its rapid expansion. More retail outlets, elaborate catwalk shows, and extravagant marketing and advertising campaigns are just some of the expensive tools the deep pockets of the big companies can fund. The really seductive proposition in selling a stake in your business to one of the big conglomerates, however, is that it fast-tracks the process and takes some of the pressure off the designer. When you don't need to worry about the light bill, you can concentrate on putting together a killer collection. With the backing of a company like Prada or LVMH, a hip fashion label can become a major global brand in a few years instead of the traditional decades. Theoretically it's a win-win situation.

Undoubtedly that's what excited the Austrian-born Helmut Lang when Prada's CEO Patrizio Bertelli (who is also the husband of Miuccia Prada, the label's designer) came knocking in 1999. Under the terms of the deal, Lang was to retain control of the design and marketing of the brand while Prada ran the business side of things, including manufacturing and distribution. It was all blue sky. Prada's expertise in leathergoods was used to launch a line of Helmut Lang accessories – shoes, bags and luggage – as well as other products such as eyewear. New stores opened throughout Asia in Hong Kong, Singapore and Tokyo, and later in other major centres such as London, Paris and Los Angeles.

So what went wrong? The decline of the brand is widely attributed to the clash between Lang and Bertelli, who wanted to take the brand in different directions. They were an unlikely pairing in the first place: Bertelli is a loud, publicity-savvy businessman, said to have a blunt and aggressive manner; Lang was known to be shy and reclusive. He rarely gave interviews and loathed the routine of runway schedules. (He once cancelled a show at the last minute and sent fashion editors a CD-ROM of his clothes instead.) When he was nominated for three major awards at the American Fashion Awards held in New York in 1999, he didn't even show up at the presentation – he was busy working in his studio downtown.

Helmut Lang was born in Vienna in 1956. His parents divorced at the age of five and he was sent to live with his grandparents in a small village in the Austrian Alps. By the time Helmut was ten, his father had remarried and the young boy moved back to Vienna to live with him and his new wife. On the day he turned eighteen he moved out of his father's house, but remained in Vienna and set out on a career as a fashion designer. Lang opened his first store in 1979 at the age of twenty-three; five years later, he closed it to concentrate on developing the label. In 1986 he showed his first women's ready-to-wear collection in Paris; menswear followed in 1987. In 1997, Lang moved his business to New York.

When Lang was designing his own label it had a certain mystique. He didn't use models in his advertisements and often didn't even feature the clothes, just the words 'Helmut Lang'. His jeans, for

example, had no visible branding on them whatsoever, yet devotees were more than happy to fork out hundreds of dollars for them. The word many fashion commentators used to describe his label at the height of its popularity was 'modern'. His minimalist aesthetic seemed to chime with the times. If 1980s fashion was all about excess and a conspicuous display of wealth, the 1990s was about hiding it.

In 2000, *Vogue* editor-in-chief Anna Wintour said in *The New Yorker*:

> Helmut came along and at first it was, 'Wait a moment, what's this? This is not in the spirit of the mid-eighties,' which was all about opulence. But then everything crashed and fashion reflected that and Helmut was there to take advantage.

The overriding aesthetic of the Prada label has been no less avant-garde than Helmut Lang and at times has also favoured a minimalist approach, but the Prada bosses cannily know how to distil that aesthetic for less adventurous consumers and commercialise it. In doing so Prada has built up a suite of brands – Miu Miu, Prada Sport/Linea Rossa and Prada – all occupying different segments of the fashion market. According to some reports Lang was uncomfortable with a similar strategy that Prada executives had put in place for his brand and didn't take kindly to being told to make the line more accessible.

Since Lang's exit from Prada he has spoken very little to the press about what happened. He has said, however, that, for the time being at least, he has no intention of getting back into the fashion business – unlike, say, Tom Ford, who since his unfortunate departure from Gucci has launched a label under his own name.

Link Theory Holdings acquired the Helmut Lang brand from Prada in 2006. Andrew Rosen, the chief executive of the American division of the company, is a third-generation ragtrader who started Theory with the designer Elie Tahari in 1996. At the time, retailers were just developing the clothing category that came to be known as 'contemporary sportswear', with the aim of satisfying the demand for more casual work clothes. In 2003 Rosen and Tahari sold the Theory label to its Japanese licensee, but Rosen retained control of the company's US subsidiary, Link Theory. Globally, Theory is now one of the dominant players in the contemporary sportswear market, with sales of US$500 million annually. At least half of that sum comes from stores in the United States – Rosen's market.

Rosen later told *The New York Times* why he felt the Helmut Lang name had promise:

> The beauty of Helmut Lang is that you had the incredible heritage and legacy, but you didn't have anything else . . . You could reshape the whole business.

NICOLE & MICHAEL COLOVOS

There was no inventory, no people, no stores. No designer either, for that matter. Rosen approached Lang about returning to work on the label he had founded, but Lang 'respectfully declined' the invitation.

So Rosen went on the hunt for a suitable designer to resurrect the label — a designer with an aesthetic similar to Lang's. In May 2006, on the recommendation of US *Vogue*'s editors, he approached Michael Colovos, then thirty-five, and his wife, Nicole, then thirty-six.

The couple had recently left Habitual, the LA-based denim label they'd founded in 2001, in circumstances that strangely echoed Lang's, so it was important to them that there was no animosity between Link Theory Holdings and the label's founder. Somewhat naively, Nicole explains:

> Helmut was approached first of all and he wasn't interested in doing it and that was important to us — that the brand hadn't been taken away from him at all. I don't know if we had his blessing, but it was his decision that he didn't want to continue with the label. It's a much nicer road for designers like us to follow, rather than it being a case of the name designer being squeezed out, as has been the case with a lot of brands.

The Colovoses certainly look the part; Nicole says they both loved the label when Lang was designing it: 'We share the same aesthetic, we were fans of the label and we both wore the clothes.'

NICOLE & MICHAEL COLOVOS

Nicole was born Nicole Garrett, in Auckland, New Zealand. She started her career as a stylist for *Elle* magazine in Sydney, but moved to New York in 1997, where she eventually found work at *Harper's Bazaar* as a market editor.

Her husband, Michael, was born and raised near Seattle and studied at the Fashion Institute of Technology in New York City. After working in Paris in the design studios of Guy Laroche he returned to the United States and established his own womenswear label called Colovos in 1998. He met Nicole when she was working at *Harper's Bazaar* in New York and came to his studio to view his collection. The couple eventually married and moved to Los Angeles, where they set up their own jeans label.

Habitual was regarded as cool and cutting edge. The pair had a good eye for streetwear and they were among the first to produce skinny leg jeans, which have been ubiquitous ever since. The label expanded into other areas such as menswear, accessories, maternity wear and children's items. When they split with Habitual's parent company, Pacific Marketing Works, in 2006, the label was said to have annual sales of about US$5 million. They have not spoken publicly about the circumstances of their departure.

Habitual had been on Andrew Rosen's radar for some time and he loved the work the Colovoses had been doing. The Habitual label often sat alongside Theory in up-market department stores around the world. Rosen therefore figured they had a good sense of what the contemporary sportswear market was all about.

The Colovoses' debut collection for Helmut Lang was for spring/ summer 2007, so they had a very short time in which to prepare. They studied the label's archive, but only lightly – giving themselves a sort of refresher course in what the label stood for. They wanted to avoid guessing what Lang might have done if he had stayed on. 'We just started looking at the archives to explore the things we loved about Helmut's work,' says Nicole.

> We are so respectful to Helmut Lang and we're not trying to recreate what he did with the label . . . What we have tried to take from him is his modernity. I just think there is a natural aesthetic that we are drawn to. There's a modern, utilitarian feel to what we are doing which is similar in spirit to what Helmut did.

They have taken the label exactly where Prada wanted to, but failed. Nicole tells me:

> What we are doing with the label is very different to the market Helmut was in. It's sitting in the higher end of the contemporary market, so it's not going to be the same designer-level pricing that Helmut Lang was known for, which was very expensive.

NICOLE & MICHAEL COLOVOS

In fashion speak, 'contemporary' is really a byword for accessible – a word no-one likes, and certainly not designers. But that's what Helmut Lang is, under its new management. It's accessible in terms of both design and price. It won't send fashion editors into a frenzy when it comes down a catwalk, but it will probably make a lot of money for its owners. Rosen acknowledged this when he spoke to *The New York Times* just before the launch of the Colovoses' debut collection. 'I want to make clothes that are accessible,' he said, 'not just so I am impressing some fashion impresario.'

Michael Colovos is nevertheless quick to point out that they are not designing the label purely just to get the tills ringing in department stores.

> We don't really think so much about repeat customers each season. Designing from a sales perspective is really bad; it's just confusing. What we are doing with the label really goes back to what we want to wear. If we suddenly find that we want a new pair of skinny jeans, or a short jacket, or we want a big oversize coat, that's going to affect our decision more than thinking about the sales end of it. We just hope that customers feel the same way.

The collection, says Michael, is more of a continuing story each season than a radical shift in direction. It is not purely trend-driven either.

We're exploring the shapes and the tailoring that will continue through every season, and over time we'll perfect them and take them to the next level. That's what will change in the clothes, more than trends.

For Nicole the decision not to be so trend-focused is reminiscent of Helmut Lang's original vision for the label. After all, as he said, quality doesn't go out of style every six months.

I just think that's how people's lifestyles are today. You can wear something like a skinny pant for several seasons and you can maybe change the proportion of what you wear it with as opposed to having to change everything that you are wearing. There is a modern, utilitarian feel to it. There will still be a certain edge to the collection each season and a certain twist, I guess, or a different take on classic pieces. Our aim is to keep it very modern and very fresh.

At the height of Helmut Lang's career his label was often thought of as the uniform of the quintessential stylish, SoHo-dwelling New Yorker. It makes sense, then, that the Colovoses moved back to New York from Los Angeles to set up their design studio for the label. Michael says:

It would have been a much more difficult task to design the label from LA than New York, because the lifestyle and the energy in New York is very different and is more suited to what we are trying to do with the label. Seeing the sorts of people walking down the street that you just don't see in Los Angeles is so much more inspiring for the type of thing we are doing now.

When I spoke with the pair, they had not yet shown their first collection. When asked if they planned on doing so with a big runway show, Michael's answer was an emphatic 'no'.

Right now there are no plans for a show and we are not necessarily working towards that either. If the collection evolves into something that requires that sort of presentation then we would look into that.

We're not really trying to make a lot of noise with this collection — we're trying to do the opposite actually. When we go shopping, we really feel there are things missing in the marketplace that we want to wear. We're just trying to make interesting clothes that we want to wear and we want to start it off small and make it quiet rather than a big huge fuss. We're going to do private showings out of our showroom and let it evolve naturally.

It's a smart strategy. A big beginning can lead to a spectacular failure if things go wrong. But now that their first few collections have been released, it doesn't look as though that's going to happen; reviews have been largely positive. In mid 2007, Laird Borrelli of Style.com wrote:

Michael and Nicole Colovos' first resort collection for Helmut Lang added a welcome edge to a season often known for its saccharine prettiness. Working in graphic black and white, the designers respected the minimalism that is the house's heritage without being limited by it. Knits, skin-exposing cutouts, and layering added texture to straight, streamlined silhouettes as well as softer, rounded ones. A pair of narrow suits were the show's highlights.

Not exactly the sort of gushing review laced with superlatives that hails a major new design talent, but nonetheless it must be music to the ears of the executives at Link Theory Holdings. Just edgy enough to get fashion-conscious consumers interested, but not so edgy that it frightens them away.

MARTIN GRANT

The rag trade is a notoriously rough business. It can bring you great riches and it can send you bankrupt. Embarking on a career in fashion can be a hard slog, too. There's the years of study and the backbreaking hours spent hunched over a sewing machine. You have to be part creative genius and part businessperson, part seamstress and part accountant, part shopkeeper and part celebrity. You need passion and patience if you want to make it to the big league.

Then again, there's always an exception to the rule, and the Australian-born designer Martin Grant definitely breaks the mould. In the early 1980s, at the age of fifteen, he dropped out of high school and set up his own atelier in the studio space of Melbourne designer Desbina Collins in Little Collins Street. By sixteen he had launched his own ready-to-wear line and by eighteen his clothes were being featured in *Vogue Australia*. At twenty he was named the Cointreau

Young Designer of the Year. In short, he was Australian fashion's Boy Wonder. In 2006, Grant was the subject of a retrospective exhibition at the Ian Potter Centre at the National Gallery of Victoria, titled 'Martin Grant, Paris'. Today, at forty years of age, he is based in Paris and is a veteran of the industry.

Despite being, arguably, this country's most successful contemporary fashion designer, most Australians have never heard of him. Collette Dinnigan, on the other hand, is widely thought to be the country's greatest designer by the average punter. Dinnigan was the first Australian designer to be invited by the Chambre Syndicale du Prêt-à-Porter des Couturiers et des Créateurs de Mode to show her collection in Paris, and her Parisienne credentials have long been cited in Australia as a sign of her success. That's not to belittle her achievements in any way — it's really just to reinforce the point that in the fashion industry buzz is everything.

Grant is more of a quiet achiever — which is exactly how *Newsweek* described him in a 2003 profile, labelling him 'fashion's quiet man'. *Time* magazine summed up his approach in a 2006 article as 'producing two collections a year with little more noise than the sound of his seamstress scissors'.

Being successful and keeping quiet in such a noisy industry is no mean feat. Today's fashion system requires designers to constantly reinvent themselves. Big retailers, such as the American department stores, demand an endless supply of new stock. In addition to the traditional spring/summer and autumn/winter collections, many designers are now doing a third so-called 'cruise' collection. Traditionally cruise collections were just that: a small range of casual clothes for women to wear on their summer holidays. Today they have become an essential component of the output of the big fashion houses, which routinely spend seven-figure sums staging elaborate catwalk shows in the US, the primary market for cruise collections. It's not so much cruise-going American women who are demanding it, but the retailers themselves. There's something of a chicken-and-egg argument happening here. Take, for example, designers who show their collections in Paris, such as Chanel or Christian Dior. They stage their spring/summer ready-to-wear shows in September for the following year's summer season. The clothes typically end up on the shop floor after the winter sales in about February. That means by the time the weather actually warms up there's nothing in the department stores for women to buy — so enter the cruise collection.

Such retail imperatives mean that a designer working for a major label must produce a minimum of three collections a year. On top of that, they have accessories and possibly even haute couture to worry about, as well as their own signature label, which may be another two collections again. The constant need to come up with something new can be exhausting. A designer has to reinvent the wheel several times a year to keep the press and buyers satisfied. Grant tends to work outside that system, making his work each season an evolution rather than a revolution, and describes himself as being part of the periphery:

> I'm definitely aware of having to make each collection feel kind of fresh and new and to keep people excited. Sometimes it's driven not by the client but by the press and the buyers, because you've got to keep them interested, to show them that you are evolving rather than just staying put, if you want critical acclaim. But I don't do extreme changes from collection to collection.

Grant's clothes are finely cut and exquisitely tailored and he shies away from an excess of surface decoration. His style is feminine without being girly and chic without being too trendy. He designs clothes that elegant women want to wear, clothes that won't look so last season if they're worn six months after they were purchased. They're also ageless.

> The appeal of my clothes is actually very broad. There are eighteen-year-old girls who wear the clothes and then there are seventy-five-year-old women who wear them too.
>
> A certain style has developed in the collections and the customer gets used to that and that's what they look for. I tend to pick out certain basics which will always come back. I will always have a trench

coat, or a pea coat, or a shirt dress. They are key items, but I think, now how can I re-work it this season so that it feels fresh and so that it feels of this season?

When I ask where he gets his inspiration, Grant is remarkably candid.

That's the most difficult question, and it's the one question that always makes me laugh . . . you know, half the time I don't know where it comes from.

Grant, somewhat pragmatically, says the starting point for each collection is the choice of fabric, because fabrics need to be chosen at least six months before he starts designing. When we spoke in March he had just returned from buying fabrics for delivery in October and admitted that he hadn't really started thinking about the collection as such, but even when choosing fabrics he says he sticks to his evolution rather than revolution mantra.

I like quite classic fabrics that I'll go back to each season, but I'm always looking for key things that will spark off the collection.

Grant says there always comes a time when he needs to get away from his office.

When I'm really starting to think about the collection I'll actually go off and – even if it's just wandering, or going to the flea market –

I'll go somewhere outside of my environment. I'll go to a gallery or a garden or a museum or something just to get me into another world. Because at work there are always one or two collections on the go at once — there's the production being done and so on and you're constantly surrounded by the previous collection, so it's quite important to get away from it.

Grant stays away from themes.

A lot of designers work with themes and I actually try to avoid that, because I think you can end up designing something that is costume-like.

For Grant's autumn/winter 2006/2007 collection, for example, he decided to visit the Louvre. He spent four days straight in the famed Paris museum and says he was particularly fond of the work of the sixteenth-century Dutch-born French painter Corneille de Lyon. He took inspiration from the artist's work — particularly in his use of colour — as well as from other artists such as Jean Auguste Dominique Ingres.

The images just sit in the back of my mind. Then I might be looking at fabric and something will click. So if I told you I'd taken inspiration from a sixteenth-century painting, you might have an idea in your head of what the collection would be. But then I've

actually mixed it with the 1960s and then just totally taken it on board and appropriated it myself, and made it my own thing. There's probably very little that you'd recognise in there as being from the sixteenth century.

Style.com picked up on this in a review of the collection. The reviewer, Nicole Phelps, made mention of the designer's sixteenth-century artistic inspiration, but noted: 'As it turns out, that obscure reference produced some very current shapes and cuts.' There were garments with teardrop-shaped sleeves, and tulip-style lapels stuffed with tulle for added volume. The collection featured some of Grant's favourite neutral colours, black and white, mixed with teal blue and hound's-tooth. It was structured, sharp and finely tailored, yet still completely feminine.

The actor Cate Blanchett has been a fan of Grant's designs for some time. She told *The Age*:

> His dresses make you look good. They do kind things to bits of your body that most women don't like, and I think that's wonderful.

Lee Radziwill, the sister of Jackie Kennedy Onassis, is another long-time fan and a permanent front-row fixture at Grant's fashion shows. In an interview with *Harper's Bazaar*, she compared Grant to the legendary Spanish designer Cristóbal Balenciaga.

Like Balenciaga, Martin understands clean lines – his cut is modern, which to me means unencumbered. I've never worn anything of his that I haven't been happy with.

Radziwill, who lives part-time in Paris, discovered Grant's designs in Barneys New York. When she couldn't find his clothes in Paris department stores she contacted him to see if she could buy from him directly. In an interview with *The Washington Post* in 2005 Grant recalled the phone call and said that when he'd clarified 'who this Radziwill woman was' he was delighted that 'someone historically associated with good taste' liked his work.

Despite Grant's quiet achiever status, the ringing support he has received from high-profile celebrities has helped him along and put him on the fashion radar. Back in 1999 Grant's fashion shows were small, low-key affairs staged in his boutique for a select group of about fifteen fashion editors and key buyers. In March 1999 US *Vogue's* editor-at-large, André Leon Talley, was one of the guests at the morning showing. (Grant held one in the morning and one in the afternoon, to be able to accommodate everyone). Talley was so taken with the collection that he convinced Naomi Campbell to model in the afternoon show for no fee. This, mind you, was the same season in which Campbell refused to model for Versace because they wouldn't pay her enough.

The supermodel's endorsement created just the right buzz. Barneys ordered the entire collection for its flagship New York store. It was the biggest single order Grant had ever received and a turning point for his business. Barneys has continued to buy Grant's collections, giving him a strong foothold in the lucrative American market, and in 2003 he was commissioned to design the department store's in-house range, called simply 'Barneys New York Collection'.

Twice a year for two to three weeks Grant goes to New York to design the Barneys collection. He says working in a different environment helps him to separate the work he does for Barneys from his own Paris-based collection.

> I like it because I am taking myself completely out of my own environment and I'm in another foreign country, a foreign environment, and looking at things that are fresh for me because I spend most of my time in Paris. But just walking around New York, you see different things and the way people dress differently, and so that has become quite important for me, to be able to separate myself from my own collection.

Grant's own line is more experimental. He is still driven by his design instincts when working for Barneys, it's just that he pushes ideas further in his personal collection. Although no collection can be designed to suit everyone, the range he designs for Barneys needs a broader appeal.

I have a fairly good idea of who my own customers are. When it comes to the Barneys collection, I tend to follow [the store's] lead on that, because the people I work with there have a very good idea of who their customer is. Occasionally I will propose something to them and they will reply with, 'No, that's too vulgar.'

Martin Grant was born in Melbourne in 1966 and grew up in the city's eastern suburbs. Grant says that his interest in fashion began at the age of five, when all his kindergarten drawings were of dresses. His grandmother Nancy Grant, a Melbourne seamstress, was a major influence on him. As soon as he could, Grant left Nunawading High School to concentrate on fashion. He was fifteen years old at the time and had not even sat his Year 10 exams – not that his failure to complete his secondary education was any sort of impediment to his success as a fashion designer. As noted above, he launched his first ready-to-wear line at just sixteen years of age, and at twenty he was named the Cointreau Young Designer of the Year.

Then, at twenty-one, and already a seasoned player in the fashion industry, he decided to give it all away.

Well, what I would say is that I got exhausted by fashion, because I started very young and it was quite intense for a few years. It was a heavy learning time and it was tiring just keeping up with it. When I got into fashion there were a lot of things that I didn't even think

about, such as the press side of it. There was a whole other side to fashion which isn't really anything to do with designing and I started to find it quite superficial and exhausting and I decided that I wanted to do something more substantial and a little deeper in its thinking. I left school so young as well, and I felt like I'd missed out on a good part of my education – which I had.

In 1987 Grant enrolled at the Victorian College of the Arts and, after a foundation year in which he studied different disciplines, he went on to complete studies in sculpture.

In a way it was testing myself. It was saying, okay, do I want to be doing this for the rest of my life – working in fashion – or try something else just to see? It was one of the best things I ever did. It made a huge difference in the way that I look at things and understand things. And at the end of it I actually came to the realisation that, you know, what I was doing was a form of sculpture. I don't pretend that what I'm doing – making fashion – is art, but there are definitely links there between the two mediums. You're working in three dimensions, you're manipulating materials, you're using historical references. I felt that in sculpture I hadn't developed a voice yet and I wasn't sure of myself and felt sort of under-confident. Whereas in fashion I had a bigger vocabulary and it made sense in a way to go back to that.

Grant made the move back to fashion in the biggest way possible. In 1990 he decided to leave Australia and play in the big league. Like many Australians, his first stop was London, where he worked at the fashion label Idol, and later with designer Koji Tatsuno, who taught him the art of bespoke tailoring.

In 1992 Grant moved to Paris to work with the German designer Anne Schramm. Schramm had been a menswear designer for Christian Dior and had decided to go out on her own. Grant designed two collections with Schramm and lasted a year in the job. By now he was in love with the world's undisputed fashion capital and decided to set up his own atelier in a disused hospital in Montmartre, which the government had turned into an authorised squat for artists.

His first ready-to-wear collections produced in the Montmartre hospital were small — about twenty pieces — but they sold quickly to buyers from Australia, Japan, the UK and the USA. By 1996 his collections had grown enough in size to enable him to open his own boutique in an old barber shop on rue des Rosiers in the Marais district.

It could have been Paris, it could have been New York, it could have been Milan or it could have been London. But in a way, Paris did attract me the most, because of its history in fashion, and it has maintained that as well. I think other major cities, they kind of go up and down, whereas Paris has always been known, and hopefully always will be known, for its creativity. In retrospect it seems obvious that I would end up there.

Today Grant's Paris boutique is still in the Marais district, but has moved to rue Charlot. His collections are also stocked in some of the world's most prestigious stores, such as Harvey Nichols and Selfridges in the UK; Barneys New York, Saks Fifth Avenue and Bloomingdale's in the United States; and Mitsukoshi in Japan, to name just a few.

Dropping out of school at the age of fifteen taught Grant an invaluable lesson in how to run a business – that the best way to learn is through trial and error. In the very early days he had an extremely basic business model:

You make a dress, you sell it, and then you can make two dresses. Then you sell two dresses and you can make four and so on. It enabled me to learn the steps as I went along rather than launching into something and borrowing lots of money to do it, because then suddenly you can find yourself in the shit and you have to know how to deal with it. It really was a kind of slow evolution, of finding out how it works. In the early days I did all the accounting, the banking, the invoicing, dealt with all the comings and goings, so that I could actually cope with it and learn. Then once it got to the big stage I already had a certain amount of experience, which was great.

That sort of level-headedness would come in handy when the talent scouts from the big fashion conglomerates started circling with their chequebooks. In recent years Grant has drawn the eye of the talent scouts at the world's biggest fashion conglomerate, Moët Hennessy–Louis Vuitton (LVMH), and in 2003 he was approached to take up the creative reins at LVMH label Celine following the departure of its designer, the American Michael Kors, who was leaving to concentrate on his own label.

It would be a dream come true for many designers: quietly toil away being a creative genius, attract the attention of the head honchos at LVMH, design collections for a prestigious luxury label, become seriously rich. But it wasn't for Grant. In late 2003 he turned LVMH down with a polite 'Thanks but no thanks.' For now, he prefers to remain in control of his own destiny.

I've always been self-financed and the business has never had any outside investors, except when I needed some financial help getting the shop open, and that's quite important to me. I like the fact that the label is autonomous and that it supports itself. I feel like what I am doing is realistic. It's not saying, okay, let's invest a couple of hundred thousand dollars and then see what return we can get on it. It's not that kind of mentality at all, it's much more — like I said — an evolution.

Not that the attention didn't have its benefits. It made his off-schedule shows a must-see on the Paris fashion calendar and earned him regular reviews in *Women's Wear Daily* and *The New York Times* for starters.

The Celine offer was not the first – or the last – that Grant has had from the big players, he says. 'They've been really interesting offers and the whole process has been interesting to go through.' He has no regrets, but insists that, if the right offer came up, designing for one of the big houses is definitely something that interests him.

> It's just been a mixture of bad timing: sometimes a question of money and my availability. You know, one of them, they actually wanted me to start and produce a collection within three to four months and for me it didn't feel right. I didn't feel that I could do a good job in the amount of time [they would have given me] and, also, that I'd be putting my own collection in jeopardy. My own collection had been developing so much in the last five years, and I didn't want to suddenly just switch over and concentrate on another label.

There were other factors too.

> You have to take into account things like who the designer was before you. Are you doing damage control? Are you walking into a situation so damaged that it's going to be difficult to do anything with it? Or if you go into a job behind someone who's been doing an incredibly

fantastic job, then you will always be compared to them. There are a lot of different factors and I'm probably particularly cautious about those things. You have to really question whether you are the right person for the job, because in a sense you're selling yourself, so you have to be sure that you're selling to the right person.

HEDI SLIMANE

I began this book by stating that no fashion designer personifies the tension between art and commerce as much as Marc Jacobs. No-one, that is, except perhaps Hedi Slimane.

Until recently — March 2007 in fact — Slimane was the artistic director of Dior Homme, the menswear branch of Christian Dior that he had built from nothing into one of the most powerful forces in men's fashion in just seven years. His departure from the brand underscored the struggle between strong-minded designers and the executives they report to.

Like Louis Vuitton, the brand Marc Jacobs designs for, Christian Dior is owned by Moët Hennessy–Louis Vuitton (LVMH). Dior is a minnow in comparison to Louis Vuitton, but is nevertheless one of the world's most successful fashion brands, generating €731 million in revenue in 2006, with profits of €56 million. Negotiations over the renewal of Slimane's contract with Dior started in July of that year and, according to reports, they were complex and tense.

At issue for Slimane, it seems, was not just the matter of remuneration, but also his creative freedom and autonomy. Slimane, according to *Women's Wear Daily*, was keen to stay on at Dior Homme, but only if LVMH agreed to back the launch of his own signature brand. That didn't happen, so he left.

It's hard to think of the shy, polite Slimane as the sort of person who relishes head-to-head negotiations. In fact, it's hard to marry the softly spoken gentleman on the phone with the high-concept punk in the photographs. Perhaps it's that French nonchalance that allows him to push for a better deal, or he'll walk.

Slimane posted a message on his website explaining why he'd quit:

> Right now I feel it is important to stay true to my principles and the idea I have about fashion. I had no other choice than to refuse the kind of proposition that was made and to decline a new Dior Homme contract.

Slimane seems indifferent to the trappings of success. Unlike Karl Lagerfeld, Valentino Garavani, or Domenico Dolce and Stefano Gabbana, he is not interested in big homes, fast cars and flashy yachts. For Slimane it's all about his uncompromising vision of fashion and how a man should dress. In an interview situation he is quiet, unassuming and very polite, but he gives the impression that for him fashion is not a career, it is his life.

Fashion is a national pastime in France, where even the taxi drivers have an opinion on the collection shows. Which makes it all the more painful that, in recent years, the heroes of the game have not been French. For most of the past decade, foreigners have been at the helm of some of the most venerable French fashion houses, driving one of the country's largest industries (second only to aviation).

The names and nationalities of those foreign invaders have passed into legend: the Englishman, John Galliano, at Christian Dior; the American, Marc Jacobs, at Louis Vuitton; the Italian, Stefano Pilati, at Yves Saint Laurent Rive Gauche; and the German, Karl Lagerfeld, at Chanel.

When Slimane joined Dior, the French had, once again, a local hero to celebrate (albeit in the rather unlikely arena of menswear, which has been considered haute couture's poor relation ever since the English and Italians perfected the art of the suit). Born and raised at the centre of the French universe, Paris, Hedi Slimane was charged, in 2000, with developing from scratch the menswear side of Christian Dior, a house that is fundamental to the French claim to pre-eminence in fashion. Except for some hopelessly daggy licensed men's products such as ties and socks, Dior was, at the time, predominantly a womenswear brand.

In just seven years, Slimane took Dior Homme from a duty-free store staple to one of the hottest men's labels in the world. The success of Dior Homme has made Slimane, together with Nicolas Ghesquière of Balenciaga, something of a Joan of Arc figure in French fashion. They have rescued their country's proud reputation as leaders in the industry and drawn the centre of the fashion industry world closer to Paris again.

Along the way Slimane defined the dominant male look of the moment. Like Dior himself, he has a happy knack of creating a style that filters down from the catwalks, through the mass-market shops and out onto the street. If, for instance, you think it was near impossible for a while to buy jeans in anything other than a narrow leg style, blame Slimane. Then there's the modified Mohawk, or cockscomb hairstyle, beloved of young men around the world — it was Slimane who wore it first.

As no less an authority than Suzy Menkes, head fashion writer at the *International Herald Tribune*, testified in July 2006: 'Slimane is a menswear designer of absolute and uncompromising vision.' (So uncompromising, in fact, that it would eventually lead him to leave his plum job as Dior Homme designer.) He has perhaps the most identifiable handwriting in fashion today. Chickadee hair and slim-cut dark-coloured jeans may have been Slimane's mainstream legacy, but it is in suiting that his approach was truly groundbreaking.

Slimane's highly structured, razor-sharp men's tailoring was the most radical thing to happen in men's fashion since Giorgio Armani took all the structure out of it in the 1970s. Where Armani made the suit relaxed and comfortable, with softer shoulders and fuller pants to flatter even an ample male posterior, Slimane put all the effort back into wearing one, with unforgivingly skinny trousers — which can make the mere task of sitting down difficult — and breathtakingly tight jackets.

The male silhouette is back, and god help you if yours has blurred slightly. Slimane's vision is relentlessly precise — and youthful:

> Tailoring is my favourite thing. It's all about the jacket . . . all about a young man in a well-cut jacket that won't look like it was stolen from his dad. I wanted to define the new jacket after the power suit of Armani. Less power and more fun, all done within luxury standards and strict tradition, but applied to a new allure and attitude.

Prior to his Dior appointment, Slimane was the menswear designer at Yves Saint Laurent, but resigned when YSL was bought by the Gucci Group in 1999 and he was faced with the prospect of reporting to Tom Ford. At YSL, efficiency and comfort were the watchwords and, says Slimane, he was told that men's clothes must be cut — among other things — to allow the wearer to drive a car. 'Who cares?' he asks disdainfully.

Men should make an effort to look better and not just the girls doing all the work to look good. Exercise exists for everyone, and you might try it before you get a suit.

Something might be lost in the translation here, but it's safe to say that Slimane believes men should suffer for fashion. Karl Lagerfeld, a close friend of Slimane, famously went on a drastic diet so that he could fit into Dior Homme and apparently existed on little more than Pepsi Max. Slimane himself denies the rumour that he stays slim by not eating. He revealed to *The New Yorker* in 2006 that he does indeed like to eat, it's just that he likes to eat baby food. He also doesn't drink, smoke or do drugs – but admires the aesthetic of those who do.

Making suits tighter and slimmer might not seem all that pioneering. After all, it's still a suit in the conventional sense and Slimane's approach is, in part, a reprise of the punk aesthetic of the 1980s. However, menswear is at heart conservative – certainly in comparison to womenswear, where the raison d'être is constant reinvention. The core of menswear, the three-piece suit, has changed very little since the industrial revolution. Men's collection shows, therefore, are a double-edged sword for designers. They are seen as either dull, staid affairs, or ridiculous: 'What man would wear that?'

Slimane says that in the twentieth century, 'we sort of went backwards in menswear'.

Taboos emerged [discouraging] the idea of perfecting men's appearance. Men's fashion until the last century was so much more sophisticated and certainly equivalent to women's fashion. Suddenly the question of sexuality emerged and it made men's fashion suspect. [It was seen as] defining [sexual] preferences. It's not a question any more, thank god.

Something has changed in men's fashion, and Slimane is responsible. While he was at Dior Homme, the label's collection shows became highly anticipated events more akin to 'happenings'. That's no accident. Slimane is as much impresario as artist. He is personally involved in casting the models who will display his clothes: unknowns Slimane scouts on the streets of London, Berlin, wherever he finds himself, often from the back of a limousine, a practice he refers to as a 'boy safari'.

Slimane prefers to use non-professional models for much the same reason that some filmmakers like to use non-professional actors – because they lend an air of authenticity to the finished product.

They just come from a different perspective than fashion models. They are true characters, usually with a strong personal style and they wear my clothes really organically. They wear them as if they could be their own clothes. We have a really good time during show preparation because they all become good friends and it ends up like a freedom territory.

When he left Dior Homme he singled his models out for praise:

They have been a strong inspiration – if not the only one – and the reason why I designed the clothes. I liked nothing more than seeing them take over the shows and making the clothes their own.

Then there's the music, which Slimane considers integral to the collection. He has commissioned alternative music stars such as Beck and the White Stripes to create original 'scores' for his shows.

Fashion for me is somewhere between social and street fashion – hedonistic party clothes. Music has been everything for me since I was six years old. It's a celebration . . . and goes with a soundtrack . . . Music is all there is. I just wouldn't do anything without it. I don't see any other thing going on creatively right now that could impact men's fashion other than music.

His own impact has been total – and radical. US *Vogue* designated him the designer pushing menswear into the future; *The New Yorker* said he had transformed the male silhouette; *GQ* went one further and said he had revolutionised manhood itself. He has even received the public imprimatur of his old boss, Yves Saint Laurent, and in a highly symbolic manner. Slimane showed his first collection for Dior Homme a day after Tom Ford showed his first collection for YSL; Saint Laurent, who had very publicly skipped Ford's show, did attend Slimane's. Afterwards, he led a standing ovation and pronounced what he had seen *formidable*.

Not that the acclaim is universal. Critics are inevitable, particularly when you are no longer the new kid on the fashion block. After Slimane's spring/summer 2007 collection show in Paris, the *New York Times* fashion writer Cathy Horyn criticised the Dior Homme designer for presenting a collection that 'betrayed an incapacity to be open to change, which is fatal in fashion'. Then again, Slimane, like other fashion radicals such as Vivienne Westwood, has a fine sense of fashion's continuity. He describes each collection as 'a chapter within the same novel. There is no rupture between seasons; it's a continuous project.'

Continuous and thoroughgoing. In addition to the clothes and shows, Slimane designed the company's atelier in Paris (featuring 200 speakers in the ceiling), and not just the Dior Homme stores but the furniture that goes in them. Beyond Dior, Slimane has created art installations for institutions such as the Architecture Foundation in London, and he's also an accomplished photographer who has published his work in two volumes, *Berlin* and *London: Birth of a Cult*, the latter documenting the live performances of rocker Pete Doherty.

In 2004, Slimane renegotiated his Dior contract to allow him the freedom to pursue creative interests beyond the house, and to be more involved in the development of the non-fashion side of the business, such as skincare and fragrance. In 2006 the company launched its first-ever men's beauty range, developed by Slimane, under the name Dior Homme Dermo System. 'They let me do the one thing I need to do: other things,' he says. (Slimane's replacement at Dior, Belgian-born designer Kris Van Assche, is responsible for ready-to-wear and accessories, but does not have control over fragrances and skincare as Slimane did – a sign, perhaps, that the era of the star designer is on the wane.)

Slimane says that although he likes to be active in many creative fields – fashion, furniture design, photography, architecture – it's all part of the same, larger project.

> It's just different languages for me, but the meaning and the ideas stay the same. I don't really have any one discipline that I prefer, although I have always had a camera in my hand since I was a child and I use it like a diary.

In 2003, *Vogue Australia* invited Slimane to undertake a photo essay on the surf culture of Sydney for its special issue guest-edited by Karl

Lagerfeld. *Vogue Australia* editor-in-chief Kirstie Clements formed a close relationship with Slimane during his time in Australia and describes him as very humble and quiet.

> I gave him carte blanche with the photographic project. I basically just left him alone and he popped into the office a couple of times for a cup of tea. We'd get reports of him wandering down [Sydney's] Oxford Street at three in the morning with his camera . . . I can't see him as being one for bureaucracy and long meetings. It doesn't surprise me that he did just throw it all in [at Dior Homme]. He will, no doubt, end up doing something else just as brilliantly.

Clements is reluctant to label Slimane a revolutionary, but says that he does have a unique take on men's fashion.

> What he has done is make the suit a young person's thing and a little less camp. It's a particular aesthetic that on the right person is so schmick you just can't improve on it. But you do have to have the right body type for it.

Clements had been aware of Slimane's work since his days at YSL and had even used some of his Dior Homme men's designs in fashion shoots for *Vogue Australia* — a women's magazine. Some of Slimane's most famous clients are, in fact, women. They include Nicole Kidman, Madonna, Catherine Deneuve and Carine Roitfeld (editor-in-chief of the French edition of *Vogue*): women who don't mind the left-over-right-side buttoning of his jackets. Clements comments:

> A brilliant black pantsuit is the ultimate thing that a woman can wear. Slimane's things are incredibly elegant and I think wearing menswear makes you feel so comfortable sometimes. It's that sense of being androgynous that can feel very comforting; that you are not being overtly feminine.

Certainly, looking at Slimane's later collections for Dior Homme there is a definite sense that many of the pieces may have been designed with a female customer in mind — a beaded bolero jacket, for example. Venturing into women's fashion while employed by Dior would have meant working in the shadow of John Galliano, the designer of the highly successful Christian Dior women's line since 1996, but there is no question that Slimane harbours a passion to design a women's line one day:

> There is a logic and an excitement to [it]. It will certainly happen no matter what, it's just a natural thing — I miss the girls.

Of course, not every woman wants to wear a mannish suit and, with women's fashion, Slimane will have to show that he knows how to design in not just two dimensions but three, something many regard as the true test of a designer. There seems little doubt he'll succeed.

Hedi Slimane grew up in the working-class Buttes-Chaumont district of Paris, the son of a Tunisian father – an accountant – and Italian mother. After high school, he studied art and began helping friends with fashion shoots and shows, acting as an art director. In 1995, while assisting at the fittings for a show by up-and-coming designer José Lévy, Slimane was spotted by the LVMH talent scout Jean-Jacques Picart, who hired him as his assistant. Picart went on to recommend Slimane for a position on Yves Saint Laurent's menswear design team in 1996. In less than a year, he had become the label's accredited designer.

When he quit YSL, Slimane was courted by a range of fashion companies that would be a dream come true for any young designer. 'It was like browsing a tourist catalogue,' he says. The Gucci Group offered him his own signature brand. Prada wanted him to take the helm at Jil Sander but offered him the chance to design his own signature brand at the same time. In the end there was one job opportunity that stood out, and in 2001, at the age of thirty-two, he settled on the task of creating a menswear line for Dior. It was, he says, a 'blank slate'.

As early as the eighteenth century the French had begun to favour English tailoring over the fancy Gallic variety. The long, slow demise of French tailoring had begun. According to Farid Chenoune in his book *A History of Men's Fashion*, in 1955 France had roughly 10,000 tailors, but by 1967 just 2000 remained. Along the way, the Italians took Savile Row to the off-the-rack masses and replaced the English as the leaders in men's tailoring. 'By the 1960s, the Italian-cut suit had become standard battle gear for a new breed of French womaniser,' Chenoune writes.

Still, menswear remained secondary to the main game, women's fashion. That began to change with the merger mania of the late 1990s. As small luxury goods companies were absorbed into huge multinational corporations, growth — the need for new categories and territories — became the new mantra, and menswear began to flourish.

'I always had the feeling you could do anything with menswear,' says Slimane.

> I never wanted to think about the gender but rather a masculine idea . . . since my debut at [YSL] I have been defining that idea of couture for men . . . my credo was to [make] younger guys [understand] tailoring as a hedonistic vocabulary and not as a status symbol or something for a wedding occasion . . . I want to make couture houses wake up and apply their tradition and techniques to menswear.

Slimane saw his work at Dior as in part political. One of his aims was to put Paris back on the map for its men's fashion — and he

succeeded. While the majority of Dior's revenue still comes from its highly successful womenswear division, menswear now represents about 10 per cent of the company's business globally, and is seen as having the potential for further growth. In 2007, LVMH chairman Bernard Arnault described the entire Dior Homme range as a 'resounding success'.

There are significant parallels between Slimane's career and that of other well-known designers. Perhaps the most striking is with that other radical French fashion designer, Pierre Cardin, who also sought to redefine the idea of the men's suit (his contribution, among other things, was to take the lapels off). Cardin, too, designed so-called unisex collections, was inspired by the emerging rock music scene — he dressed the Beatles — and liked to cast unknown models, in his case French students. In July 2007, Cardin showed his first collection in years — and it was menswear.

In the lengthy message that Slimane posted on his website after his resignation from Dior Homme he wrote:

> I always kept in mind the precedence of some designers I admire who were in a similar situation and chose the other path.

No doubt he was referring to Jil Sander and Helmut Lang, who both sold majority stakes in their fashion houses to the Prada Group only to end up clashing with management and ultimately leaving their signature brands. But he is also not the first designer to lose the job of a lifetime only to go onto even greater success. His previous employer, Yves Saint Laurent, started his career working for Dior in Paris, just like Slimane. He was just seventeen. When Dior died in 1957, Saint Laurent was put in charge at the age of twenty-one. In 1961 Saint Laurent was unceremoniously dumped from the house of Dior and went on to establish his own label, which would later become a legendary critical and commercial success. Like his former boss, it seems likely Slimane will go on to greater things.

Reflecting on history, however, is not something that Slimane often does.

It's so important to live in the present and not to miss your time. To live it, experience it, and participate in it. I'm not interested in nostalgia. I'm more interested in what creates the moment. That's what fashion asks: 'What is today?'

# LIST OF ILLUSTRATIONS